2012 | THE LITTLE DATA BOOK ON EXTERNAL DEBT

THE WORLD BANK

ISBN: 978-0-8213-8999-7
eISBN: 978-0-8213-9520-2
DOI: 10.1596/978-0-8213-8999-7
SKU: 18999

The Little Data Book on External Debt 2012
is a product of the Development Data Group of the
Development Economics Vice Presidency of the World Bank.

Design by Communications Development Incorporated, Washington, D.C.
Cover design by Peter Grundy Art & Design, London, U.K.

Contents

Acknowledgments

The Little Data Book on External Debt was prepared by the Financial Data Team of the Development Data Group (DECDG), led by Ibrahim Levent under the supervision of Neil James Fantom, and comprising Nanasamudd Chhim, Akane Hanai, Wendy Huang, Hiroko Maeda, Gloria Moreno, Evis Rucaj, Yasue Sakuramoto, Sun Hwa Song, Rubena Sukaj, Maryna Taran, and Alagiriswamy Venkatesan, working closely with other teams in the Development Economics Vice Presidency's Development Data Group. The team was assisted by Awatif H. Abuzeid and Elysee Kiti. The system support team was led by Abdolreza Farivari. The Migration and Remittances unit provided worker remittances and compensation of employee data. Many others within the World Bank provided helpful input, including country economists who reviewed the data. The work was carried out under the management of Ms. Shaida Badiee.

The production of this volume was managed by Azita Amjadi with the assistance of Alison Kwong and Jomo Tariku. The CD-ROM and online database were prepared by Shelley Fu and William Prince, with technical support from Ramgopal Erabelly and Malarvizhi Veerappan. Mobile apps production was coordinated by Vilas K. Madlekar and Parastoo Oloumi. Staff from External Affairs coordinated the publication and dissemination of the book.

Foreword

The Little Data Book on External Debt, a pocket edition of *Global Development Finance 2012: External Debt of Developing Countries,* contains statistical tables on the external debt of the 129 countries that report public and publicly guaranteed external debt under the Debtor Reporting System. It also includes tables of selected debt and resource flow statistics for individual reporting countries as well as summary tables for regional and income groups. It is the culmination of a year-long process that requires extensive cooperation from people and organizations around the globe—national central banks, ministries of finance, major multilateral organizations, and many departments of the World Bank.

The Little Data Book on External Debt provides a quick reference for users of the *Global Development Finance 2012* book, CD-ROM, and online database. The general cutoff date for data is September 2011.

The Little Data Book on External Debt covers external debt stocks and flows, major economic aggregates, key debt ratios, and the currency composition of long-term external debt for all countries reporting through the Debtor Reporting System. Terms used in tables are defined in the *Glossary*.

The economic aggregates presented in the tables are prepared for the convenience of users. Although debt ratios can provide useful information about developments in debt-servicing capacity, drawing valid conclusions from them requires careful economic evaluation.

The macroeconomic information is from standard sources, but much of it is subject to considerable margins of error, and the usual care must be taken in interpreting the indicators. This is particularly the case for the most recent year, for which figures are preliminary and subject to revision. All the relevant data and information are available to you from the World Bank's Open Data site at http://data.worldbank.org/.

Shaida Badiee
Director
Development Data Group

Data notes

Unless otherwise indicated, all data are in millions of U.S. dollars.

The following symbols are used throughout the tables:

0 or 0.0   means zero or small enough that the number would round to zero at the displayed number of decimal places.

..   means that data are not available or that aggregates cannot be calculated because of missing data in the years shown.

$ indicates current U.S. dollars unless otherwise specified.

Converting to a common currency

Debt data are normally reported to the World Bank in the currency of repayment. To produce summary tables, these data have to be converted to a common currency (U.S. dollars). Because flow data are converted at average annual exchange rates and stock data at year-end exchange rates, year to year changes in debt outstanding and disbursed are sometimes not equal to net flows (disbursements less principal repayments). Similarly, changes in debt outstanding, including undisbursed debt, differ from commitments less repayments. Discrepancies are particularly large when exchange rates have moved sharply during the year; cancellations and reschedulings of other liabilities into long-term public debt also contribute to the differences.

Regional tables

The country composition of regions is based on the World Bank's analytical regions and may differ from common geographic usage.

East Asia and Pacific

Cambodia (A), China (P), Fiji (A), Indonesia (A), Lao PDR (P), Malaysia (E), Mongolia (A), Myanmar (E), Papua New Guinea (A), Philippines (A), Samoa (A), Solomon Islands (A), Thailand (A), Tonga (A), Vanuatu (E), Vietnam (P).

Europe and Central Asia

Albania (A), Armenia (A), Azerbaijan (A), Belarus (A), Bosnia and Herzegovina (A), Bulgaria (A), Georgia (A), Kazakhstan (A), Kosovo (A), Kyrgyz Republic (A), Latvia (A), Lithuania (A), Macedonia, FYR (A), Moldova (A), Montenegro (A), Romania (A), Russian Federation (P), Serbia (A), Tajikistan (A), Turkey (A), Turkmenistan (E), Ukraine (A), Uzbekistan (A).

Latin America and the Caribbean

Argentina (A), Belize (A), Bolivia (A), Brazil (A), Chile (A), Colombia (A), Costa Rica (A), Dominica (A), Dominican Republic (A), Ecuador (A), El Salvador (A), Grenada (A), Guatemala (A), Guyana (A), Haiti (A), Honduras (A), Jamaica (A), Mexico (A), Nicaragua (A), Panama (A), Paraguay (A), Peru (A), St. Kitts and Nevis (A), St. Lucia (A), St. Vincent and the Grenadines (A), Uruguay (A), Venezuela, RB (A).

Middle East and North Africa

Algeria (A), Djibouti (A), Egypt, Arab Rep. (A), Iran, Islamic Rep. (A), Jordan (A), Lebanon (A), Morocco (A), Syrian Arab Republic (A), Tunisia (A), Yemen, Republic of (A).

South Asia

Afghanistan (A), Bangladesh (A), Bhutan (A), India (A), Maldives (A), Nepal (A), Pakistan (A), Sri Lanka (A).

Sub-Saharan Africa

Angola (A), Benin (A), Botswana (A), Burkina Faso (A), Burundi (P), Cameroon (A), Cape Verde (A), Central African Republic (P), Chad (A), Comoros (A), Congo, Dem. Rep. (E), Congo, Rep. (E), Côte d'Ivoire (E), Eritrea (E), Ethiopia (A), Gabon (A), Gambia, The (A), Ghana (A), Guinea (E), Guinea-Bissau (E), Kenya (A), Lesotho (A), Liberia (A), Madagascar (A), Malawi (A), Mali (A), Mauritania (A), Mauritius (A), Mozambique (A), Niger (A), Nigeria (A), Rwanda (A), São Tomé and Príncipe (A), Senegal (A), Seychelles (A), Sierra Leone (A), Somalia (E), South Africa (P), Sudan (A), Swaziland (A), Tanzania (A), Togo (A), Uganda (A), Zambia (P), Zimbabwe (A).

Note: Letters in parentheses indicate reporters' Debtor Reporting System status: (A) as reported, (P) preliminary, and (E) estimated. *As reported* indicates that the country was fully current in its reporting under the Debtor Reporting System and that World Bank staff are satisfied that the reported data give an adequate and fair representation of the country's total external debt. *Preliminary* data are based on reported or collected information but, because of incompleteness or other reasons, an element of staff estimation is included. *Estimated* data indicate that countries are not current in their reporting and that a significant element of staff estimation has been necessary in producing the data tables.

All developing countries

Present value of external debt	3,689,003
Population (millions)	5,631
External debt per capita ($)	723.9
Share of public sector external debt in total (%)	38.5

	2009	2010
External debt stocks	3,639,595	4,076,298
Long-term external debt	2,813,091	2,975,259
Public and publicly guaranteed	1,477,075	1,582,586
Official creditors	772,345	822,575
Private creditors	704,730	760,010
Bonds	484,388	527,752
Private nonguaranteed	1,336,016	1,392,674
Use of International Monetary Fund (IMF) credit	53,298	64,661
Short-term external debt	773,206	1,036,378
Interest in arrears on long-term external debt	26,428	21,090
Disbursements	534,464	655,672
Long-term external debt	505,843	638,831
Public and publicly guaranteed	217,405	253,309
IMF purchases	28,621	16,842
Principal repayments	383,041	428,917
Long-term external debt	381,197	425,895
Public and publicly guaranteed	117,318	124,527
IMF repurchases	1,844	3,022
Net flows on external debt	166,167	495,230
Short-term external debt	14,744	268,474
Interest payments	125,886	154,434
Long-term external debt	111,244	111,949
Public and publicly guaranteed	54,237	55,120
IMF charges	571	986
Short-term external debt	14,071	41,499
Net transfers	40,282	340,796
Total external debt service paid	508,927	583,351
Other non-debt resource inflows		
Net flow of long-term external debt (excluding IMF)	124,646	212,936
Foreign direct investment	399,950	506,062
Portfolio equity	108,756	128,413
Major economic aggregates		
Gross national income (GNI)	16,264,212	19,437,081
Exports of goods, services and income	4,727,932	5,936,528
Workers' remittances & compensation of employees	306,271	319,552
Profit remittances on FDI	319,275	342,894
Ratios (%)		
External debt stocks to exports	77	69
External debt stocks to GNI	22	21
External debt service to exports	11	10
Present value of external debt to exports	..	68
Present value of external debt to GNI	..	21
Reserves to external debt stocks	133	137
Currency Composition (%)		
Euro	14.1	12.7
Japanese yen	10.1	10.4
U.S. dollar	67.9	69.4

East Asia & Pacific

Present value of external debt		932,277
Population (millions)		1,936
External debt per capita ($)		523.8
Share of public sector external debt in total (%)		29.8

	2009	2010
External debt stocks	833,821	1,013,971
Long-term external debt	506,653	545,176
Public and publicly guaranteed	294,848	306,774
Official creditors	201,669	207,769
Private creditors	93,179	99,005
Bonds	60,812	67,184
Private nonguaranteed	211,805	238,402
Use of International Monetary Fund (IMF) credit	291	271
Short-term external debt	326,877	468,525
Interest in arrears on long-term external debt	1,226	1,338
Disbursements	88,027	123,095
Long-term external debt	87,853	123,062
Public and publicly guaranteed	38,112	41,164
IMF purchases	174	33
Principal repayments	82,541	85,742
Long-term external debt	82,490	85,694
Public and publicly guaranteed	24,895	26,291
IMF repurchases	50	48
Net flows on external debt	68,968	178,890
Short-term external debt	63,481	141,537
Interest payments	18,701	47,087
Long-term external debt	14,303	18,042
Public and publicly guaranteed	9,419	10,524
IMF charges	2	2
Short-term external debt	4,397	29,042
Net transfers	50,267	131,803
Total external debt service paid	101,242	132,828
Other non-debt resource inflows		
Net flow of lung-term external debt (excluding IMF)	5,363	37,368
Foreign direct investment	137,453	227,709
Portfolio equity	28,868	40,463
Major economic aggregates		
Gross national income (GNI)	6,347,846	7,530,404
Exports of goods, services and income	2,101,318	2,741,865
Workers' remittances & compensation of employees	85,963	91,959
Profit remittances on FDI	117,556	122,031
Ratios (%)		
External debt stocks to exports	40	37
External debt stocks to GNI	13	13
External debt service to exports	5	5
Present value of external debt to exports	..	38
Present value of external debt to GNI	..	14
Reserves to external debt stocks	339	333
Currency Composition (%)		
Euro	6.6	5.7
Japanese yen	24.6	25.5
U.S. dollar	62.8	63.0

Europe & Central Asia

Present value of external debt	1,135,629
Population (millions)	405
External debt per capita ($)	3,143.5
Share of public sector external debt in total (%)	28.6

	2009	2010
External debt stocks	1,212,410	1,273,418
Long-term external debt	987,057	994,159
Public and publicly guaranteed	330,536	366,663
Official creditors	94,097	104,968
Private creditors	236,439	261,695
Bonds	133,579	156,088
Private nonguaranteed	656,521	627,496
Use of International Monetary Fund (IMF) credit	36,222	45,027
Short-term external debt	189,131	234,232
Interest in arrears on long-term external debt	1,890	1,461
Disbursements	215,289	248,650
Long-term external debt	193,895	237,021
Public and publicly guaranteed	63,105	73,519
IMF purchases	21,394	11,629
Principal repayments	165,077	206,788
Long-term external debt	164,143	204,517
Public and publicly guaranteed	28,047	31,622
IMF repurchases	935	2,271
Net flows on external debt	11,689	87,393
Short-term external debt	−38,523	45,531
Interest payments	49,767	46,433
Long-term external debt	44,530	40,530
Public and publicly guaranteed	13,414	13,455
IMF charges	454	818
Short-term external debt	4,784	5,085
Net transfers	−38,078	40,960
Total external debt service paid	214,845	253,220
Other non-debt resource inflows		
Net flow of long-term external debt (excluding IMF)	29,753	32,505
Foreign direct investment	85,927	86,268
Portfolio equity	6,367	−846
Major economic aggregates		
Gross national income (GNI)	2,540,148	2,963,163
Exports of goods, services and income	862,023	1,047,760
Workers' remittances & compensation of employees	36,079	36,037
Profit remittances on FDI	60,831	79,212
Ratios (%)		
External debt stocks to exports	141	122
External debt stocks to GNI	48	43
External debt service to exports	25	24
Present value of external debt to exports	..	109
Present value of external debt to GNI	..	39
Reserves to external debt stocks	56	59
Currency Composition (%)		
Euro	21.6	21.5
Japanese yen	2.9	2.9
U.S. dollar	73.0	73.1

Latin America & Caribbean

Present value of external debt		987,607
Population (millions)		571
External debt per capita ($)		1,820.1
Share of public sector external debt in total (%)		43.7

	2009	2010
External debt stocks	899,103	1,038,725
Long-term external debt	751,466	828,184
Public and publicly guaranteed	429,963	457,714
Official creditors	149,159	169,259
Private creditors	280,804	288,456
Bonds	240,414	238,992
Private nonguaranteed	321,503	370,470
Use of International Monetary Fund (IMF) credit	1,243	2,265
Short-term external debt	146,393	208,277
Interest in arrears on long-term external debt	11,672	6,374
Disbursements	155,204	193,616
Long-term external debt	154,754	192,157
Public and publicly guaranteed	68,601	75,403
IMF purchases	450	1,459
Principal repayments	96,857	96,088
Long-term external debt	96,804	95,937
Public and publicly guaranteed	36,765	41,193
IMF repurchases	53	151
Net flows on external debt	53,821	164,709
Short-term external debt	−4,526	67,182
Interest payments	41,265	44,157
Long-term external debt	38,344	38,914
Public and publicly guaranteed	21,952	22,102
IMF charges	9	17
Short-term external debt	2,912	5,227
Net transfers	12,556	120,552
Total external debt service paid	138,122	140,246
Other non-debt resource inflows		
Net flow of long-term external debt (excluding IMF)	57,951	96,220
Foreign direct investment	78,321	112,626
Portfolio equity	41,582	41,300
Major economic aggregates		
Gross national income (GNI)	3,866,338	4,786,771
Exports of goods, services and income	821,954	1,017,266
Workers' remittances & compensation of employees	56,572	57,245
Profit remittances on FDI	77,457	88,845
Ratios (%)		
External debt stocks to exports	109	102
External debt stocks to GNI	23	22
External debt service to exports	17	14
Present value of external debt to exports	..	103
Present value of external debt to GNI	..	23
Reserves to external debt stocks	62	62
Currency Composition (%)		
Euro	11.1	8.9
Japanese yen	4.0	4.4
U.S. dollar	82.1	84.5

Middle East & North Africa

Present value of external debt	123,417
Population (millions)	289
External debt per capita ($)	497.3
Share of public sector external debt in total (%)	78.6

	2009	2010
External debt stocks	141,010	143,595
Long-term external debt	118,411	119,872
Public and publicly guaranteed	112,261	113,766
Official creditors	77,734	77,550
Private creditors	34,527	36,216
Bonds	23,544	26,825
Private nonguaranteed	6,150	6,106
Use of International Monetary Fund (IMF) credit	200	195
Short-term external debt	22,400	23,528
Interest in arrears on long-term external debt	326	342
Disbursements	13,668	14,586
Long-term external debt	13,666	14,533
Public and publicly guaranteed	12,071	13,236
IMF purchases	2	53
Principal repayments	13,283	12,189
Long-term external debt	13,220	12,135
Public and publicly guaranteed	10,990	10,304
IMF repurchases	64	54
Net flows on external debt	1,949	3,509
Short-term external debt	1,564	1,112
Interest payments	4,961	4,927
Long-term external debt	4,361	4,263
Public and publicly guaranteed	4,100	4,048
IMF charges	3	2
Short-term external debt	597	662
Net transfers	-3,012	-1,417
Total external debt service paid	18,244	17,116
Other non-debt resource inflows		
Net flow of long-term external debt (excluding IMF)	446	2,398
Foreign direct investment	26,079	22,670
Portfolio equity	1,200	36
Major economic aggregates		
Gross national income (GNI)	926,767	1,018,299
Exports of goods, services and income	328,128	337,580
Workers' remittances & compensation of employees	32,412	31,016
Profit remittances on FDI	13,957	3,595
Ratios (%)		
External debt stocks to exports	43	43
External debt stocks to GNI	15	14
External debt service to exports	6	5
Present value of external debt to exports	..	46
Present value of external debt to GNI	..	13
Reserves to external debt stocks	214	227
Currency Composition (%)		
Euro	32.2	30.5
Japanese yen	8.4	8.8
U.S. dollar	41.5	42.5

South Asia

Present value of external debt		331,209
Population (millions)		1,579
External debt per capita ($)		253.6
Share of public sector external debt in total (%)		48.5

	2009	2010
External debt stocks	353,417	400,596
Long-term external debt	292,199	325,804
Public and publicly guaranteed	169,387	194,376
Official creditors	145,635	155,989
Private creditors	23,751	38,387
Bonds	12,671	23,980
Private nonguaranteed	122,812	131,428
Use of International Monetary Fund (IMF) credit	9,081	10,913
Short-term external debt	52,137	63,879
Interest in arrears on long-term external debt	47	100
Disbursements	39,248	52,398
Long-term external debt	35,271	50,074
Public and publicly guaranteed	17,874	30,691
IMF purchases	3,978	2,325
Principal repayments	15,585	19,891
Long-term external debt	15,228	19,541
Public and publicly guaranteed	8,713	8,876
IMF repurchases	356	349
Net flows on external debt	26,304	44,161
Short-term external debt	2,640	11,653
Interest payments	7,223	7,469
Long-term external debt	6,460	6,493
Public and publicly guaranteed	2,688	2,767
IMF charges	76	140
Short-term external debt	687	836
Net transfers	19,081	36,692
Total external debt service paid	22,808	27,360
Other non-debt resource inflows		
Net flow of long-term external debt (excluding IMF)	20,043	30,532
Foreign direct investment	39,404	27,960
Portfolio equity	20,541	39,447
Major economic aggregates		
Gross national income (GNI)	1,705,510	2,090,779
Exports of goods, services and income	328,149	424,897
Workers' remittances & compensation of employees	75,063	82,209
Profit remittances on FDI	16,197	17,147
Ratios (%)		
External debt stocks to exports	108	94
External debt stocks to GNI	21	19
External debt service to exports	7	6
Present value of external debt to exports	..	87
Present value of external debt to GNI	..	19
Reserves to external debt stocks	89	84
Currency Composition (%)		
Euro	6.0	4.9
Japanese yen	18.3	18.4
U.S. dollar	57.7	60.4

Sub-Saharan Africa

Present value of external debt		178,864
Population (millions)		851
External debt per capita ($)		242.0
Share of public sector external debt in total (%)		69.6

	2009	2010
External debt stocks	199,834	205,992
Long-term external debt	157,305	162,065
Public and publicly guaranteed	140,080	143,293
Official creditors	104,051	107,041
Private creditors	36,030	36,252
Bonds	13,368	14,684
Private nonguaranteed	17,224	18,772
Use of International Monetary Fund (IMF) credit	6,261	5,991
Short-term external debt	36,269	37,936
Interest in arrears on long-term external debt	11,266	11,474
Disbursements	23,027	23,327
Long-term external debt	20,404	21,983
Public and publicly guaranteed	17,640	19,294
IMF purchases	2,623	1,344
Principal repayments	9,698	8,219
Long-term external debt	9,313	8,070
Public and publicly guaranteed	7,908	6,240
IMF repurchases	385	149
Net flows on external debt	3,437	16,568
Short-term external debt	−9,893	1,460
Interest payments	3,968	4,362
Long-term external debt	3,246	3,707
Public and publicly guaranteed	2,664	2,225
IMF charges	28	8
Short-term external debt	694	647
Net transfers	−532	12,206
Total external debt service paid	13,666	12,581
Other non-debt resource inflows		
Net flow of long-term external debt (excluding IMF)	11,091	13,913
Foreign direct investment	32,765	28,828
Portfolio equity	10,198	8,014
Major economic aggregates		
Gross national income (GNI)	891,648	1,030,221
Exports of goods, services and income	302,759	381,839
Workers' remittances & compensation of employees	20,183	21,087
Profit remittances on FDI	33,276	32,065
Ratios (%)		
External debt stocks to exports	66	54
External debt stocks to GNI	22	20
External debt service to exports	5	3
Present value of external debt to exports	..	46
Present value of external debt to GNI	..	19
Reserves to external debt stocks	78	75
Currency Composition (%)		
Euro	18.9	15.1
Japanese yen	3.2	2.4
U.S. dollar	54.0	56.8

Income group tables

For operational and analytical purposes the World Bank's main criterion for classifying economies is gross national income (GNI) per capita. Each economy in *The Little Book on External Debt* is classified as low income or middle income. Low- and middle-income economies are sometimes referred to as developing economies. The use of the term is convenient; it is not intended to imply that all economies in the group are experiencing similar development or that other economies have reached a preferred or final stage of development. Classification by income does not necessarily reflect development status.

Low-income economies are those with a GNI per capita of $1,005 or less in 2010.

Middle-income economies are those with a GNI per capita of more than $1,006 but less than $12,275. Lower-middle-income and upper-middle-income economies are separated at a GNI per capita of $3,976.

Low income

Present value of external debt		75,766
Population (millions)		772
External debt per capita ($)		151.0
Share of public sector external debt in total (%)		82.2

	2009	2010
External debt stocks	119,669	116,593
Long-term external debt	103,185	99,631
Public and publicly guaranteed	100,165	95,929
Official creditors	96,110	92,057
Private creditors	4,056	3,871
Bonds	0	0
Private nonguaranteed	3,019	3,703
Use of International Monetary Fund (IMF) credit	5,304	4,156
Short-term external debt	11,181	12,806
Interest in arrears on long-term external debt	5,292	5,651
Disbursements	11,278	10,664
Long-term external debt	9,774	9,919
Public and publicly guaranteed	8,993	8,189
IMF purchases	1,505	745
Principal repayments	3,041	4,064
Long-term external debt	2,747	3,870
Public and publicly guaranteed	2,057	2,705
IMF repurchases	293	194
Net flows on external debt	7,259	7,832
Short-term external debt	–979	1,232
Interest payments	1,187	1,137
Long-term external debt	1,047	1,008
Public and publicly guaranteed	977	885
IMF charges	31	5
Short-term external debt	110	125
Net transfers	6,072	6,695
Total external debt service paid	4,228	5,201
Other non-debt resource inflows		
Net flow of long-term external debt (excluding IMF)	7,026	6,049
Foreign direct investment	9,231	12,716
Portfolio equity	–2	–52
Major economic aggregates		
Gross national income (GNI)	378,964	409,271
Exports of goods, services and income	89,832	108,309
Workers' remittances & compensation of employees	22,555	24,553
Profit remittances on FDI	2,799	2,134
Ratios (%)		
External debt stocks to exports	133	108
External debt stocks to GNI	32	28
External debt service to exports	5	5
Present value of external debt to exports	..	98
Present value of external debt to GNI	..	24
Reserves to external debt stocks	35	36
Currency Composition (%)		
Euro	9.3	6.7
Japanese yen	9.7	8.2
U.S. dollar	49.7	50.2

Middle income

Present value of external debt		3,613,237
Population (millions)		4,859
External debt per capita ($)		814.9
Share of public sector external debt in total (%)		37.2

	2009	2010
External debt stocks	3,519,926	3,959,705
Long-term external debt	2,709,906	2,875,628
Public and publicly guaranteed	1,376,910	1,486,657
Official creditors	676,235	730,518
Private creditors	700,675	756,139
Bonds	484,388	527,752
Private nonguaranteed	1,332,997	1,388,971
Use of International Monetary Fund (IMF) credit	47,994	60,505
Short-term external debt	762,026	1,023,572
Interest in arrears on long-term external debt	21,136	15,439
Disbursements	523,186	645,008
Long-term external debt	496,070	628,912
Public and publicly guaranteed	208,412	245,119
IMF purchases	27,117	16,097
Principal repayments	380,000	424,853
Long-term external debt	378,450	422,024
Public and publicly guaranteed	115,261	121,822
IMF repurchases	1,550	2,829
Net flows on external debt	158,908	487,398
Short-term external debt	15,723	267,243
Interest payments	124,699	153,298
Long-term external debt	110,197	110,942
Public and publicly guaranteed	53,260	54,235
IMF charges	541	982
Short-term external debt	13,961	41,374
Net transfers	34,210	334,101
Total external debt service paid	504,699	578,151
Other non-debt resource inflows		
Net flow of long-term external debt (excluding IMF)	117,620	206,887
Foreign direct investment	390,719	493,345
Portfolio equity	108,757	128,465
Major economic aggregates		
Gross national income (GNI)	15,873,869	19,009,329
Exports of goods, services and income	4,640,317	5,829,275
Workers' remittances & compensation of employees	283,716	294,999
Profit remittances on FDI	316,476	340,760
Ratios (%)		
External debt stocks to exports	76	68
External debt stocks to GNI	22	21
External debt service to exports	11	10
Present value of external debt to exports	..	67
Present value of external debt to GNI	..	21
Reserves to external debt stocks	136	140
Currency Composition (%)		
Euro	14.5	13.0
Japanese yen	10.1	10.5
U.S. dollar	69.2	70.7

Country tables

China

Data for China do not include data for Hong Kong SAR, China; Macao SAR, China; or Taiwan, China.

Serbia and Montenegro

Montenegro declared independence from Serbia and Montenegro on June 3, 2006. This edition of *The Little Data Book on External Debt* lists data for Serbia and Montenegro separately.

Tanzania

Data for Tanzania include data for Zanzibar.

Afghanistan

South Asia	Low income
Present value of external debt	721
Population (thousands)	34,385.1
External debt per capita ($)	66.8
Share of public sector external debt in total (%)	90.4

	2009	2010
External debt stocks	2,223	2,297
Long-term external debt	2,097	2,076
Public and publicly guaranteed	2,097	2,076
Official creditors	2,096	2,076
Private creditors	0	0
Bonds	0	0
Private nonguaranteed	0	0
Use of International Monetary Fund (IMF) credit	106	119
Short-term external debt	20	102
Interest in arrears on long-term external debt	20	67
Disbursements	126	87
Long-term external debt	109	79
Public and publicly guaranteed	109	79
IMF purchases	17	9
Principal repayments	3	1
Long-term external debt	3	1
Public and publicly guaranteed	3	1
IMF repurchases	0	0
Net flows on external debt	123	86
Short-term external debt	0	0
Interest payments	7	8
Long-term external debt	7	7
Public and publicly guaranteed	7	7
IMF charges	1	0
Short-term external debt	0	1
Net transfers	116	78
Total external debt service paid	10	9
Other non-debt resource inflows		
Foreign direct investment	185	76
Portfolio equity	..	..
Major economic aggregates		
Gross national income (GNI)	..	..
Exports of goods, services and income	..	..
Workers' remittances & compensation of employees	..	..
Profit remittances on FDI	..	..
Ratios (%)		
External debt stocks to exports	..	..
External debt stocks to GNI	..	..
External debt service to exports	..	..
Present value of external debt to exports	..	21
Present value of external debt to GNI	..	6
Reserves to external debt stocks	..	..
Currency Composition (%)		
Euro	0.0	0.0
Japanese yen	0.0	0.0
U.S. dollar	69.1	59.8

Albania

Present value of external debt	3,616
Population (millions)	3.2
External debt per capita ($)	1,477.9
Share of public sector external debt in total (%)	62.7

	2009	2010
External debt stocks	4,693	4,736
Long-term external debt	3,786	4,105
Public and publicly guaranteed	2,803	2,972
Official creditors	2,132	2,159
Private creditors	671	813
Bonds	0	401
Private nonguaranteed	983	1,133
Use of International Monetary Fund (IMF) credit	71	58
Short-term external debt	835	573
Interest in arrears on long-term external debt	0	0
Disbursements	753	825
Long-term external debt	750	825
Public and publicly guaranteed	559	631
IMF purchases	4	0
Principal repayments	135	379
Long-term external debt	121	367
Public and publicly guaranteed	80	346
IMF repurchases	14	12
Net flows on external debt	523	184
Short-term external debt	–95	–262
Interest payments	91	85
Long-term external debt	80	77
Public and publicly guaranteed	69	65
IMF charges	1	0
Short-term external debt	11	8
Net transfers	432	99
Total external debt service paid	227	464
Other non-debt resource inflows		
Foreign direct investment	964	1,110
Portfolio equity	3	8
Major economic aggregates		
Gross national income (GNI)	11,936	11,681
Exports of goods, services and income	3,908	4,169
Workers' remittances & compensation of employees	1,317	1,156
Profit remittances on FDI	436	362
Ratios (%)		
External debt stocks to exports	120	114
External debt stocks to GNI	39	41
External debt service to exports	6	11
Present value of external debt to exports	..	88
Present value of external debt to GNI	..	30
Reserves to external debt stocks	50	54
Currency Composition (%)		
Euro	54.9	57.0
Japanese yen	2.1	2.2
U.S. dollar	33.6	30.8

Algeria

Middle East & North Africa	Upper middle income
Present value of external debt	4,687
Population (millions)	35.5
External debt per capita ($)	148.8
Share of public sector external debt in total (%)	45.1

	2009	2010
External debt stocks	5,424	5,276
Long-term external debt	3,932	3,498
Public and publicly guaranteed	2,950	2,530
Official creditors	2,020	1,805
Private creditors	930	726
Bonds	0	0
Private nonguaranteed	982	968
Use of International Monetary Fund (IMF) credit	0	0
Short-term external debt	1,492	1,778
Interest in arrears on long-term external debt	0	0
Disbursements	194	30
Long-term external debt	194	30
Public and publicly guaranteed	71	28
IMF purchases	0	0
Principal repayments	879	573
Long-term external debt	879	573
Public and publicly guaranteed	357	339
IMF repurchases	0	0
Net flows on external debt	−496	−257
Short-term external debt	189	286
Interest payments	139	111
Long-term external debt	121	93
Public and publicly guaranteed	72	62
IMF charges	0	0
Short-term external debt	18	18
Net transfers	−634	−368
Total external debt service paid	1,017	684
Other non-debt resource inflows		
Foreign direct investment	2,760	2,291
Portfolio equity	..	..
Major economic aggregates		
Gross national income (GNI)	139,577	155,538
Exports of goods, services and income	52,917	65,400
Workers' remittances & compensation of employees	2,059	2,044
Profit remittances on FDI	5,892	..
Ratios (%)		
External debt stocks to exports	10	8
External debt stocks to GNI	4	3
External debt service to exports	2	1
Present value of external debt to exports	..	5
Present value of external debt to GNI	..	3
Reserves to external debt stocks	2,860	3,231
Currency Composition (%)		
Euro	59.7	57.3
Japanese yen	4.4	4.9
U.S. dollar	30.1	31.6

Angola

Sub-Saharan Africa	Lower middle income
Present value of external debt	15,787
Population (millions)	19.1
External debt per capita ($)	972.8
Share of public sector external debt in total (%)	83.2

	2009	2010
External debt stocks	16,616	18,562
Long-term external debt	13,629	15,440
Public and publicly guaranteed	13,629	15,440
Official creditors	4,814	8,152
Private creditors	8,814	7,287
Bonds	0	0
Private nonguaranteed	0	0
Use of International Monetary Fund (IMF) credit	359	882
Short-term external debt	2,629	2,241
Interest in arrears on long-term external debt	85	68
Disbursements	4,146	4,454
Long-term external debt	3,793	3,930
Public and publicly guaranteed	3,793	3,930
IMF purchases	353	524
Principal repayments	3,130	2,109
Long-term external debt	3,130	2,109
Public and publicly guaranteed	3,130	2,109
IMF repurchases	0	0
Net flows on external debt	1,212	1,974
Short-term external debt	196	−371
Interest payments	423	200
Long-term external debt	392	164
Public and publicly guaranteed	392	164
IMF charges	0	6
Short-term external debt	31	30
Net transfers	788	1,774
Total external debt service paid	3,554	2,309
Other non-debt resource inflows		
Foreign direct investment	2,205	..
Portfolio equity	..	..
Major economic aggregates		
Gross national income (GNI)	68,671	75,516
Exports of goods, services and income	41,582	51,375
Workers' remittances & compensation of employees	0	0
Profit remittances on FDI	6,130	0
Ratios (%)		
External debt stocks to exports	40	36
External debt stocks to GNI	24	25
External debt service to exports	9	4
Present value of external debt to exports	..	22
Present value of external debt to GNI	..	22
Reserves to external debt stocks	82	106
Currency Composition (%)		
Euro	9.7	8.6
Japanese yen	0.0	0.0
U.S. dollar	88.5	89.9

Argentina

Latin America & Caribbean		Upper middle income
Present value of external debt		121,281
Population (millions)		40.4
External debt per capita ($)		3,163.6
Share of public sector external debt in total (%)		52.6

	2009	2010
External debt stocks	120,283	127,849
Long-term external debt	100,651	92,844
Public and publicly guaranteed	72,927	67,331
Official creditors	22,333	22,922
Private creditors	50,595	44,409
Bonds	49,670	43,571
Private nonguaranteed	27,723	25,514
Use of International Monetary Fund (IMF) credit	0	0
Short-term external debt	19,632	35,005
Interest in arrears on long-term external debt	10,760	5,457
Disbursements	7,537	6,845
Long-term external debt	7,537	6,845
Public and publicly guaranteed	3,591	2,545
IMF purchases	0	0
Principal repayments	8,784	10,444
Long-term external debt	8,784	10,444
Public and publicly guaranteed	3,071	4,789
IMF repurchases	0	0
Net flows on external debt	–2,350	17,078
Short-term external debt	–1,102	20,676
Interest payments	3,343	3,596
Long-term external debt	3,222	3,426
Public and publicly guaranteed	1,887	2,337
IMF charges	0	0
Short-term external debt	121	170
Net transfers	–5,692	13,482
Total external debt service paid	12,127	14,040
Other non-debt resource inflows		
Foreign direct investment	4,017	6,337
Portfolio equity	–212	–208
Major economic aggregates		
Gross national income (GNI)	297,639	353,713
Exports of goods, services and income	70,254	84,079
Workers' remittances & compensation of employees	621	641
Profit remittances on FDI	8,360	8,516
Ratios (%)		
External debt stocks to exports	171	152
External debt stocks to GNI	40	36
External debt service to exports	17	17
Present value of external debt to exports	..	150
Present value of external debt to GNI	..	37
Reserves to external debt stocks	40	41
Currency Composition (%)		
Euro	36.0	31.2
Japanese yen	2.7	3.1
U.S. dollar	58.8	63.8

Armenia

Europe & Central Asia	Lower middle income
Present value of external debt	4,687
Population (millions)	3.1
External debt per capita ($)	1,973.7
Share of public sector external debt in total (%)	41.9

	2009	2010
External debt stocks	4,886	6,103
Long-term external debt	3,778	4,744
Public and publicly guaranteed	2,376	2,557
Official creditors	2,375	2,556
Private creditors	1	1
Bonds	0	0
Private nonguaranteed	1,401	2,187
Use of International Monetary Fund (IMF) credit	587	741
Short-term external debt	521	618
Interest in arrears on long-term external debt	0	0
Disbursements	1,713	1,919
Long-term external debt	1,247	1,734
Public and publicly guaranteed	941	198
IMF purchases	466	184
Principal repayments	323	879
Long-term external debt	300	857
Public and publicly guaranteed	21	24
IMF repurchases	23	22
Net flows on external debt	1,458	1,137
Short-term external debt	68	97
Interest payments	100	89
Long-term external debt	79	60
Public and publicly guaranteed	23	35
IMF charges	4	8
Short-term external debt	17	21
Net transfers	1,358	1,048
Total external debt service paid	423	968
Other non-debt resource inflows		
Foreign direct investment	777	570
Portfolio equity	1	0
Major economic aggregates		
Gross national income (GNI)	8,708	9,424
Exports of goods, services and income	2,054	2,897
Workers' remittances & compensation of employees	769	996
Profit remittances on FDI	332	364
Ratios (%)		
External debt stocks to exports	238	211
External debt stocks to GNI	56	65
External debt service to exports	21	33
Present value of external debt to exports	..	183
Present value of external debt to GNI	..	46
Reserves to external debt stocks	41	31
Currency Composition (%)		
Euro	6.3	5.8
Japanese yen	11.3	14.6
U.S. dollar	66.0	62.8

Azerbaijan

Europe & Central Asia		Upper middle income
Present value of external debt		3,894
Population (millions)		9.0
External debt per capita ($)		770.7
Share of public sector external debt in total (%)		55.8

	2009	2010
External debt stocks	4,531	6,974
Long-term external debt	3,660	6,050
Public and publicly guaranteed	3,346	3,892
Official creditors	2,178	2,665
Private creditors	1,168	1,226
Bonds	0	0
Private nonguaranteed	314	2,158
Use of International Monetary Fund (IMF) credit	62	46
Short-term external debt	810	878
Interest in arrears on long-term external debt	0	0
Disbursements	870	2,780
Long-term external debt	870	2,780
Public and publicly guaranteed	820	866
IMF purchases	0	0
Principal repayments	264	315
Long-term external debt	246	300
Public and publicly guaranteed	193	228
IMF repurchases	19	15
Net flows on external debt	247	2,532
Short-term external debt	−359	68
Interest payments	83	95
Long-term external debt	64	75
Public and publicly guaranteed	52	62
IMF charges	0	0
Short-term external debt	19	20
Net transfers	164	2,437
Total external debt service paid	347	410
Other non-debt resource inflows		
Foreign direct investment	473	563
Portfolio equity	0	1
Major economic aggregates		
Gross national income (GNI)	40,255	46,870
Exports of goods, services and income	23,398	29,216
Workers' remittances & compensation of employees	1,274	1,432
Profit remittances on FDI	3,664	3,815
Ratios (%)		
External debt stocks to exports	19	24
External debt stocks to GNI	11	15
External debt service to exports	1	1
Present value of external debt to exports	..	14
Present value of external debt to GNI	..	9
Reserves to external debt stocks	118	92
Currency Composition (%)		
Euro	27.0	28.9
Japanese yen	12.7	13.8
U.S. dollar	51.3	49.4

Bangladesh

South Asia	Low income
Present value of external debt	15,886
Population (millions)	148.7
External debt per capita ($)	167.9
Share of public sector external debt in total (%)	85.6

	2009	2010
External debt stocks	23,802	24,963
Long-term external debt	21,187	21,371
Public and publicly guaranteed	21,187	21,371
Official creditors	21,103	21,303
Private creditors	84	69
Bonds	0	0
Private nonguaranteed	0	0
Use of International Monetary Fund (IMF) credit	675	617
Short-term external debt	1,940	2,974
Interest in arrears on long-term external debt	1	2
Disbursements	1,499	963
Long-term external debt	1,499	963
Public and publicly guaranteed	1,499	963
IMF purchases	0	0
Principal repayments	727	780
Long-term external debt	703	734
Public and publicly guaranteed	703	734
IMF repurchases	23	46
Net flows on external debt	818	1,216
Short-term external debt	46	1,033
Interest payments	228	233
Long-term external debt	197	199
Public and publicly guaranteed	197	199
IMF charges	6	3
Short-term external debt	25	32
Net transfers	591	983
Total external debt service paid	954	1,013
Other non-debt resource inflows		
Foreign direct investment	713	968
Portfolio equity	−153	..
Major economic aggregates		
Gross national income (GNI)	97,485	109,438
Exports of goods, services and income	17,098	21,765
Workers' remittances & compensation of employees	10,521	10,852
Profit remittances on FDI	1,105	1,164
Ratios (%)		
External debt stocks to exports	139	115
External debt stocks to GNI	24	23
External debt service to exports	6	5
Present value of external debt to exports	..	84
Present value of external debt to GNI	..	16
Reserves to external debt stocks	43	45
Currency Composition (%)		
Euro	0.6	0.5
Japanese yen	9.0	9.8
U.S. dollar	53.5	52.7

Belarus

Europe & Central Asia	Upper middle income
Present value of external debt	23,088
Population (millions)	9.5
External debt per capita ($)	2,710.7
Share of public sector external debt in total (%)	30.5

	2009	2010
External debt stocks	17,490	25,726
Long-term external debt	6,594	10,251
Public and publicly guaranteed	4,823	7,850
Official creditors	4,694	5,882
Private creditors	128	1,968
Bonds	0	1,802
Private nonguaranteed	1,772	2,401
Use of International Monetary Fund (IMF) credit	2,871	3,495
Short-term external debt	8,024	11,980
Interest in arrears on long-term external debt	3	0
Disbursements	4,980	5,675
Long-term external debt	2,154	5,007
Public and publicly guaranteed	1,265	3,628
IMF purchases	2,825	668
Principal repayments	866	905
Long-term external debt	866	905
Public and publicly guaranteed	158	163
IMF repurchases	0	0
Net flows on external debt	5,178	8,729
Short-term external debt	1,064	3,959
Interest payments	313	506
Long-term external debt	172	239
Public and publicly guaranteed	105	154
IMF charges	13	66
Short-term external debt	128	201
Net transfers	4,865	8,223
Total external debt service paid	1,179	1,411
Other non-debt resource inflows		
Foreign direct investment	1,884	1,403
Portfolio equity	1	1
Major economic aggregates		
Gross national income (GNI)	49,507	54,989
Exports of goods, services and income	25,341	30,400
Workers' remittances & compensation of employees	358	376
Profit remittances on FDI	872	1,039
Ratios (%)		
External debt stocks to exports	69	85
External debt stocks to GNI	35	47
External debt service to exports	5	5
Present value of external debt to exports	..	75
Present value of external debt to GNI	..	42
Reserves to external debt stocks	32	20
Currency Composition (%)		
Euro	7.7	15.8
Japanese yen	0.0	0.2
U.S. dollar	89.4	70.5

Belize

Latin America & Caribbean	Lower middle income
Present value of external debt	784
Population (thousands)	344.7
External debt per capita ($)	3,032.7
Share of public sector external debt in total (%)	97.3

	2009	2010
External debt stocks	1,071	1,045
Long-term external debt	1,054	1,031
Public and publicly guaranteed	1,040	1,021
Official creditors	417	406
Private creditors	624	615
Bonds	21	21
Private nonguaranteed	14	10
Use of International Monetary Fund (IMF) credit	7	7
Short-term external debt	10	7
Interest in arrears on long-term external debt	10	7
Disbursements	78	31
Long-term external debt	71	31
Public and publicly guaranteed	71	31
IMF purchases	7	0
Principal repayments	53	53
Long-term external debt	53	53
Public and publicly guaranteed	51	49
IMF repurchases	0	0
Net flows on external debt	25	−22
Short-term external debt	0	0
Interest payments	46	48
Long-term external debt	46	48
Public and publicly guaranteed	45	47
IMF charges	0	0
Short-term external debt	0	0
Net transfers	−21	−70
Total external debt service paid	99	101
Other non-debt resource inflows		
Foreign direct investment	109	96
Portfolio equity	..	..
Major economic aggregates		
Gross national income (GNI)	1,236	1,303
Exports of goods, services and income	733	834
Workers' remittances & compensation of employees	80	80
Profit remittances on FDI	56	102
Ratios (%)		
External debt stocks to exports	146	125
External debt stocks to GNI	87	80
External debt service to exports	14	12
Present value of external debt to exports	..	96
Present value of external debt to GNI	..	63
Reserves to external debt stocks	20	21
Currency Composition (%)		
Euro	1.5	1.3
Japanese yen	0.0	0.0
U.S. dollar	97.2	97.5

Benin

Sub-Saharan Africa		Low income
Present value of external debt		852
Population (millions)		8.8
External debt per capita ($)		138.0
Share of public sector external debt in total (%)		92.9

	2009	2010
External debt stocks	1,072	1,221
Long-term external debt	990	1,134
Public and publicly guaranteed	990	1,134
Official creditors	990	1,134
Private creditors	0	0
Bonds	0	0
Private nonguaranteed	0	0
Use of International Monetary Fund (IMF) credit	39	55
Short-term external debt	44	32
Interest in arrears on long-term external debt	32	25
Disbursements	166	209
Long-term external debt	150	193
Public and publicly guaranteed	150	193
IMF purchases	16	16
Principal repayments	25	30
Long-term external debt	25	30
Public and publicly guaranteed	25	30
IMF repurchases	0	0
Net flows on external debt	120	175
Short-term external debt	−21	−5
Interest payments	12	13
Long-term external debt	12	13
Public and publicly guaranteed	12	13
IMF charges	0	0
Short-term external debt	0	0
Net transfers	108	162
Total external debt service paid	37	43
Other non-debt resource inflows		
Foreign direct investment	134	111
Portfolio equity	9	..
Major economic aggregates		
Gross national income (GNI)	6,605	6,633
Exports of goods, services and income	1,489	..
Workers' remittances & compensation of employees	251	248
Profit remittances on FDI	32	0
Ratios (%)		
External debt stocks to exports	72	..
External debt stocks to GNI	16	18
External debt service to exports	2	..
Present value of external debt to exports	..	70
Present value of external debt to GNI	..	13
Reserves to external debt stocks	115	98
Currency Composition (%)		
Euro	5.3	9.7
Japanese yen	0.0	0.0
U.S. dollar	21.5	19.9

Bhutan

Present value of external debt	714
Population (thousands)	725.9
External debt per capita ($)	1,237.3
Share of public sector external debt in total (%)	99.3

	2009	2010
External debt stocks	751.9	898.2
Long-term external debt	746.9	892.2
Public and publicly guaranteed	746.9	892.2
Official creditors	746.9	892.2
Private creditors	0.0	0.0
Bonds	0.0	0.0
Private nonguaranteed	0.0	0.0
Use of International Monetary Fund (IMF) credit	0.0	0.0
Short-term external debt	5.0	6.0
Interest in arrears on long-term external debt	0.0	0.0
Disbursements	91.9	177.8
Long-term external debt	91.9	177.8
Public and publicly guaranteed	91.9	177.8
IMF purchases	0.0	0.0
Principal repayments	41.1	46.6
Long-term external debt	41.1	46.6
Public and publicly guaranteed	41.1	46.6
IMF repurchases	0.0	0.0
Net flows on external debt	47.8	132.2
Short-term external debt	–3.0	1.0
Interest payments	34.4	37.6
Long-term external debt	34.4	37.5
Public and publicly guaranteed	34.4	37.5
IMF charges	0.0	0.0
Short-term external debt	0.0	0.1
Net transfers	13.4	94.7
Total external debt service paid	75.5	84.2
Other non-debt resource inflows		
Foreign direct investment	17.6	11.7
Portfolio equity	..	..
Major economic aggregates		
Gross national income (GNI)	1,229.6	1,419.7
Exports of goods, services and income	534.8	..
Workers' remittances & compensation of employees	4.8	4.8
Profit remittances on FDI	1.1	..
Ratios (%)		
External debt stocks to exports	141	..
External debt stocks to GNI	61	63
External debt service to exports	14	..
Present value of external debt to exports	..	87
Present value of external debt to GNI	..	55
Reserves to external debt stocks	118	112
Currency Composition (%)		
Euro	11.5	10.1
Japanese yen	0.0	3.3
U.S. dollar	24.0	22.3

Bolivia, Plurinational State of

Latin America & Caribbean		Lower middle income
Present value of external debt		2,999
Population (millions)		9.9
External debt per capita ($)		530.4
Share of public sector external debt in total (%)		53.1

	2009	2010
External debt stocks	5,743	5,267
Long-term external debt	5,189	5,164
Public and publicly guaranteed	2,542	2,806
Official creditors	2,451	2,782
Private creditors	92	24
Bonds	0	0
Private nonguaranteed	2,647	2,358
Use of International Monetary Fund (IMF) credit	0	0
Short-term external debt	554	103
Interest in arrears on long-term external debt	0	0
Disbursements	512	552
Long-term external debt	512	552
Public and publicly guaranteed	415	522
IMF purchases	0	0
Principal repayments	453	567
Long-term external debt	453	567
Public and publicly guaranteed	196	246
IMF repurchases	0	0
Net flows on external debt	455	–467
Short-term external debt	396	–451
Interest payments	138	79
Long-term external debt	119	76
Public and publicly guaranteed	71	53
IMF charges	0	0
Short-term external debt	19	4
Net transfers	317	–546
Total external debt service paid	592	647
Other non-debt resource inflows		
Foreign direct investment	423	622
Portfolio equity	0	0
Major economic aggregates		
Gross national income (GNI)	16,666	18,926
Exports of goods, services and income	5,666	6,922
Workers' remittances & compensation of employees	1,069	1,088
Profit remittances on FDI	769	863
Ratios (%)		
External debt stocks to exports	101	76
External debt stocks to GNI	34	28
External debt service to exports	10	9
Present value of external debt to exports	..	41
Present value of external debt to GNI	..	17
Reserves to external debt stocks	149	185
Currency Composition (%)		
Euro	3.1	2.7
Japanese yen	0.0	0.0
U.S. dollar	82.0	84.8

Bosnia and Herzegovina

Europe & Central Asia	Upper middle income
Present value of external debt	6,716
Population (millions)	3.8
External debt per capita ($)	2,249.2
Share of public sector external debt in total (%)	44.3

	2009	2010
External debt stocks	9,625	8,457
Long-term external debt	7,662	6,899
Public and publicly guaranteed	3,570	3,751
Official creditors	3,043	3,285
Private creditors	527	466
Bonds	322	273
Private nonguaranteed	4,091	3,149
Use of International Monetary Fund (IMF) credit	286	521
Short-term external debt	1,677	1,037
Interest in arrears on long-term external debt	0	0
Disbursements	683	771
Long-term external debt	401	534
Public and publicly guaranteed	329	464
IMF purchases	282	237
Principal repayments	510	1,128
Long-term external debt	510	1,128
Public and publicly guaranteed	109	145
IMF repurchases	0	0
Net flows on external debt	945	–997
Short-term external debt	772	–640
Interest payments	290	231
Long-term external debt	217	177
Public and publicly guaranteed	63	55
IMF charges	1	5
Short-term external debt	72	49
Net transfers	655	–1,228
Total external debt service paid	800	1,359
Other non-debt resource inflows		
Foreign direct investment	240	232
Portfolio equity	0	0
Major economic aggregates		
Gross national income (GNI)	17,630	17,317
Exports of goods, services and income	6,360	6,819
Workers' remittances & compensation of employees	2,133	1,905
Profit remittances on FDI	–70	27
Ratios (%)		
External debt stocks to exports	151	124
External debt stocks to GNI	55	49
External debt service to exports	13	20
Present value of external debt to exports	..	95
Present value of external debt to GNI	..	37
Reserves to external debt stocks	47	52
Currency Composition (%)		
Euro	48.6	51.0
Japanese yen	1.2	1.3
U.S. dollar	32.8	30.8

Botswana

Sub-Saharan Africa	Upper middle income
Present value of external debt	1,141
Population (millions)	2.0
External debt per capita ($)	851.4
Share of public sector external debt in total (%)	79.1

	2009	2010
External debt stocks	1,617	1,709
Long-term external debt	1,388	1,352
Public and publicly guaranteed	1,388	1,352
Official creditors	1,387	1,351
Private creditors	2	1
Bonds	0	0
Private nonguaranteed	0	0
Use of International Monetary Fund (IMF) credit	0	0
Short-term external debt	229	357
Interest in arrears on long-term external debt	0	0
Disbursements	1,006	17
Long-term external debt	1,006	17
Public and publicly guaranteed	1,006	17
IMF purchases	0	0
Principal repayments	36	56
Long-term external debt	36	56
Public and publicly guaranteed	36	56
IMF repurchases	0	0
Net flows on external debt	1,156	89
Short-term external debt	186	128
Interest payments	11	19
Long-term external debt	9	16
Public and publicly guaranteed	9	16
IMF charges	0	0
Short-term external debt	2	4
Net transfers	1,146	70
Total external debt service paid	47	75
Other non-debt resource inflows		
Foreign direct investment	252	529
Portfolio equity	18	0
Major economic aggregates		
Gross national income (GNI)	11,514	14,771
Exports of goods, services and income	4,531	5,094
Workers' remittances & compensation of employees	88	100
Profit remittances on FDI	727	..
Ratios (%)		
External debt stocks to exports	36	34
External debt stocks to GNI	14	12
External debt service to exports	1	1
Present value of external debt to exports	..	19
Present value of external debt to GNI	..	9
Reserves to external debt stocks	538	461
Currency Composition (%)		
Euro	2.0	0.3
Japanese yen	3.5	3.6
U.S. dollar	7.7	8.1

Brazil

Latin America & Caribbean	Upper middle income
Present value of external debt	326,721
Population (millions)	194.9
External debt per capita ($)	1,779.9
Share of public sector external debt in total (%)	26.9

	2009	2010
External debt stocks	276,910	346,978
Long-term external debt	237,121	281,482
Public and publicly guaranteed	87,295	96,542
Official creditors	32,385	41,251
Private creditors	54,910	55,290
Bonds	47,107	41,323
Private nonguaranteed	149,826	184,940
Use of International Monetary Fund (IMF) credit	0	0
Short-term external debt	39,789	65,496
Interest in arrears on long-term external debt	3	4
Disbursements	57,670	84,723
Long-term external debt	57,670	84,723
Public and publicly guaranteed	13,727	19,301
IMF purchases	0	0
Principal repayments	30,425	31,972
Long-term external debt	30,425	31,972
Public and publicly guaranteed	7,740	9,573
IMF repurchases	0	0
Net flows on external debt	30,386	78,458
Short-term external debt	3,142	25,706
Interest payments	14,165	13,835
Long-term external debt	13,675	13,150
Public and publicly guaranteed	5,778	5,166
IMF charges	0	0
Short-term external debt	489	684
Net transfers	16,222	64,623
Total external debt service paid	44,590	45,806
Other non-debt resource inflows		
Foreign direct investment	25,949	48,438
Portfolio equity	37,071	37,684
Major economic aggregates		
Gross national income (GNI)	1,562,412	2,049,172
Exports of goods, services and income	189,549	241,089
Workers' remittances & compensation of employees	4,234	4,000
Profit remittances on FDI	21,029	26,584
Ratios (%)		
External debt stocks to exports	146	144
External debt stocks to GNI	18	17
External debt service to exports	24	19
Present value of external debt to exports	..	146
Present value of external debt to GNI	..	19
Reserves to external debt stocks	86	83
Currency Composition (%)		
Euro	7.2	6.1
Japanese yen	5.0	5.0
U.S. dollar	84.2	86.0

Bulgaria

Europe & Central Asia	Upper middle income
Present value of external debt	44,915
Population (millions)	7.5
External debt per capita ($)	6,373.5
Share of public sector external debt in total (%)	9.3

	2009	2010
External debt stocks	53,499	48,077
Long-term external debt	34,921	32,704
Public and publicly guaranteed	4,772	4,466
Official creditors	3,322	3,152
Private creditors	1,450	1,314
Bonds	1,430	1,301
Private nonguaranteed	30,148	28,238
Use of International Monetary Fund (IMF) credit	0	0
Short-term external debt	18,578	15,373
Interest in arrears on long-term external debt	0	0
Disbursements	8,191	1,499
Long-term external debt	8,191	1,499
Public and publicly guaranteed	520	200
IMF purchases	0	0
Principal repayments	3,694	3,381
Long-term external debt	3,694	3,381
Public and publicly guaranteed	281	268
IMF repurchases	0	0
Net flows on external debt	4,740	−5,087
Short-term external debt	244	−3,205
Interest payments	1,516	634
Long-term external debt	773	568
Public and publicly guaranteed	211	160
IMF charges	0	0
Short-term external debt	743	66
Net transfers	3,224	−5,721
Total external debt service paid	5,210	4,014
Other non-debt resource inflows		
Foreign direct investment	3,389	2,168
Portfolio equity	8	9
Major economic aggregates		
Gross national income (GNI)	46,900	45,871
Exports of goods, services and income	24,392	28,358
Workers' remittances & compensation of employees	1,592	1,387
Profit remittances on FDI	1,822	1,964
Ratios (%)		
External debt stocks to exports	219	170
External debt stocks to GNI	114	105
External debt service to exports	21	14
Present value of external debt to exports	..	159
Present value of external debt to GNI	..	95
Reserves to external debt stocks	35	36
Currency Composition (%)		
Euro	56.8	56.1
Japanese yen	12.4	14.4
U.S. dollar	30.4	29.2

Burkina Faso

Sub-Saharan Africa	Low income
Present value of external debt	1,538
Population (millions)	16.5
External debt per capita ($)	124.7
Share of public sector external debt in total (%)	93.7

	2009	2010
External debt stocks	1,822	2,053
Long-term external debt	1,711	1,925
Public and publicly guaranteed	1,711	1,925
Official creditors	1,690	1,907
Private creditors	22	18
Bonds	0	0
Private nonguaranteed	0	0
Use of International Monetary Fund (IMF) credit	110	129
Short-term external debt	0	0
Interest in arrears on long-term external debt	0	0
Disbursements	266	296
Long-term external debt	212	274
Public and publicly guaranteed	212	274
IMF purchases	54	21
Principal repayments	27	33
Long-term external debt	27	32
Public and publicly guaranteed	27	32
IMF repurchases	0	1
Net flows on external debt	129	263
Short-term external debt	–110	0
Interest payments	15	18
Long-term external debt	15	18
Public and publicly guaranteed	15	18
IMF charges	0	0
Short-term external debt	0	0
Net transfers	114	245
Total external debt service paid	42	51
Other non-debt resource inflows		
Foreign direct investment	105	37
Portfolio equity	..	..
Major economic aggregates		
Gross national income (GNI)	8,019	8,810
Exports of goods, services and income	1,140	..
Workers' remittances & compensation of employees	99	95
Profit remittances on FDI	35	0
Ratios (%)		
External debt stocks to exports	160	..
External debt stocks to GNI	23	23
External debt service to exports	4	..
Present value of external debt to exports	..	169
Present value of external debt to GNI	..	19
Reserves to external debt stocks	71	52
Currency Composition (%)		
Euro	12.6	12.2
Japanese yen	0.0	0.0
U.S. dollar	35.4	33.6

Burundi

Sub-Saharan Africa		Low income
Present value of external debt		194
Population (millions)		8.4
External debt per capita ($)		64.1
Share of public sector external debt in total (%)		76.7

	2009	2010
External debt stocks	512.7	537.1
Long-term external debt	414.7	411.7
Public and publicly guaranteed	414.7	411.7
Official creditors	414.7	411.7
Private creditors	0.0	0.0
Bonds	0.0	0.0
Private nonguaranteed	0.0	0.0
Use of International Monetary Fund (IMF) credit	90.9	109.6
Short-term external debt	7.1	15.8
Interest in arrears on long-term external debt	0.1	0.8
Disbursements	43.9	55.8
Long-term external debt	23.6	35.6
Public and publicly guaranteed	23.6	35.6
IMF purchases	20.4	20.1
Principal repayments	15.3	1.8
Long-term external debt	8.4	1.8
Public and publicly guaranteed	8.4	1.8
IMF repurchases	6.9	0.0
Net flows on external debt	21.6	62.0
Short-term external debt	−7.0	8.0
Interest payments	4.1	1.6
Long-term external debt	3.6	1.4
Public and publicly guaranteed	3.6	1.4
IMF charges	0.4	0.0
Short-term external debt	0.1	0.1
Net transfers	17.5	60.4
Total external debt service paid	19.5	3.4
Other non-debt resource inflows		
Foreign direct investment	0.3	0.8
Portfolio equity	0.0	0.0
Major economic aggregates		
Gross national income (GNI)	1,331.3	1,589.0
Exports of goods, services and income	117.3	..
Workers' remittances & compensation of employees	28.2	28.2
Profit remittances on FDI	8.1	10.1
Ratios (%)		
External debt stocks to exports	437	..
External debt stocks to GNI	39	34
External debt service to exports	17	..
Present value of external debt to exports	..	151
Present value of external debt to GNI	..	14
Reserves to external debt stocks	63	62
Currency Composition (%)		
Euro	17.1	9.3
Japanese yen	3.0	3.0
U.S. dollar	34.1	37.2

Cambodia

East Asia & Pacific		Low income
Present value of external debt		3,652
Population (millions)		14.1
External debt per capita ($)		330.7
Share of public sector external debt in total (%)		94.4

	2009	2010
External debt stocks	4,364	4,676
Long-term external debt	4,099	4,414
Public and publicly guaranteed	4,099	4,414
Official creditors	4,099	4,414
Private creditors	0	0
Bonds	0	0
Private nonguaranteed	0	0
Use of International Monetary Fund (IMF) credit	0	0
Short-term external debt	265	262
Interest in arrears on long-term external debt	208	215
Disbursements	211	347
Long-term external debt	211	347
Public and publicly guaranteed	211	347
IMF purchases	0	0
Principal repayments	26	33
Long-term external debt	26	33
Public and publicly guaranteed	26	33
IMF repurchases	0	0
Net flows on external debt	116	303
Short-term external debt	−69	−10
Interest payments	23	29
Long-term external debt	22	28
Public and publicly guaranteed	22	28
IMF charges	0	0
Short-term external debt	1	1
Net transfers	92	274
Total external debt service paid	49	62
Other non-debt resource inflows		
Foreign direct investment	530	783
Portfolio equity	0	..
Major economic aggregates		
Gross national income (GNI)	9,962	10,779
Exports of goods, services and income	5,982	..
Workers' remittances & compensation of employees	338	369
Profit remittances on FDI	349	..
Ratios (%)		
External debt stocks to exports	73	..
External debt stocks to GNI	44	43
External debt service to exports	1	..
Present value of external debt to exports	..	59
Present value of external debt to GNI	..	36
Reserves to external debt stocks	75	82
Currency Composition (%)		
Euro	0.9	0.8
Japanese yen	2.4	2.8
U.S. dollar	40.6	41.2

Cameroon

Sub-Saharan Africa	Lower middle income
Present value of external debt	1,194
Population (millions)	19.6
External debt per capita ($)	151.2
Share of public sector external debt in total (%)	73.7

	2009	2010
External debt stocks	2,946	2,964
Long-term external debt	2,748	2,762
Public and publicly guaranteed	2,132	2,185
Official creditors	2,122	2,169
Private creditors	10	15
Bonds	0	0
Private nonguaranteed	615	577
Use of International Monetary Fund (IMF) credit	175	172
Short-term external debt	23	31
Interest in arrears on long-term external debt	23	31
Disbursements	491	278
Long-term external debt	344	278
Public and publicly guaranteed	135	278
IMF purchases	147	0
Principal repayments	336	155
Long-term external debt	336	155
Public and publicly guaranteed	107	117
IMF repurchases	0	0
Net flows on external debt	155	122
Short-term external debt	0	0
Interest payments	59	53
Long-term external debt	58	53
Public and publicly guaranteed	27	38
IMF charges	0	0
Short-term external debt	0	0
Net transfers	96	70
Total external debt service paid	395	208
Other non-debt resource inflows		
Foreign direct investment	668	–1
Portfolio equity	0	0
Major economic aggregates		
Gross national income (GNI)	22,059	22,030
Exports of goods, services and income	5,550	5,738
Workers' remittances & compensation of employees	192	195
Profit remittances on FDI	436	166
Ratios (%)		
External debt stocks to exports	53	52
External debt stocks to GNI	13	13
External debt service to exports	7	4
Present value of external debt to exports	..	19
Present value of external debt to GNI	..	5
Reserves to external debt stocks	125	123
Currency Composition (%)		
Euro	63.5	54.8
Japanese yen	0.0	0.3
U.S. dollar	14.2	18.7

Cape Verde

Sub-Saharan Africa		Lower middle income
Present value of external debt		455
Population (thousands)		496.0
External debt per capita ($)		1,728.5
Share of public sector external debt in total (%)		98.8

	2009	2010
External debt stocks	706.8	857.3
Long-term external debt	694.3	847.3
Public and publicly guaranteed	694.3	847.3
Official creditors	687.8	794.8
Private creditors	6.5	52.5
Bonds	0.0	0.0
Private nonguaranteed	0.0	0.0
Use of International Monetary Fund (IMF) credit	11.0	8.6
Short-term external debt	1.5	1.5
Interest in arrears on long-term external debt	1.5	1.5
Disbursements	97.3	192.1
Long-term external debt	97.3	192.1
Public and publicly guaranteed	97.3	192.1
IMF purchases	0.0	0.0
Principal repayments	26.9	27.9
Long-term external debt	25.4	25.6
Public and publicly guaranteed	25.4	25.6
IMF repurchases	1.5	2.3
Net flows on external debt	70.4	164.3
Short-term external debt	0.0	0.0
Interest payments	7.0	7.9
Long-term external debt	6.9	7.9
Public and publicly guaranteed	6.9	7.9
IMF charges	0.1	0.0
Short-term external debt	0.0	0.0
Net transfers	63.4	156.3
Total external debt service paid	33.9	35.8
Other non-debt resource inflows		
Foreign direct investment	119.8	111.4
Portfolio equity	1.8	0.0
Major economic aggregates		
Gross national income (GNI)	1,543.6	1,578.9
Exports of goods, services and income	603.0.	668.8
Workers' remittances & compensation of employees	138.1	138.6
Profit remittances on FDI	26.3	..
Ratios (%)		
External debt stocks to exports	117	128
External debt stocks to GNI	46	54
External debt service to exports	6	5
Present value of external debt to exports	..	72
Present value of external debt to GNI	..	29
Reserves to external debt stocks	56	45
Currency Composition (%)		
Euro	19.0	25.7
Japanese yen	0.2	1.0
U.S. dollar	43.4	38.3

Central African Republic

Sub-Saharan Africa		Low income
Present value of external debt		246
Population (millions)		4.4
External debt per capita ($)		87.4
Share of public sector external debt in total (%)		56.6

	2009	2010
External debt stocks	394.1	384.8
Long-term external debt	236.7	217.8
Public and publicly guaranteed	236.7	217.8
Official creditors	202.3	183.6
Private creditors	34.4	34.2
Bonds	0.0	0.0
Private nonguaranteed	0.0	0.0
Use of International Monetary Fund (IMF) credit	78.4	90.4
Short-term external debt	79.0	76.6
Interest in arrears on long-term external debt	75.0	74.6
Disbursements	44.4	19.3
Long-term external debt	4.8	6.0
Public and publicly guaranteed	4.8	6.0
IMF purchases	39.6	13.2
Principal repayments	27.7	1.0
Long-term external debt	8.4	1.0
Public and publicly guaranteed	8.4	1.0
IMF repurchases	19.4	0.0
Net flows on external debt	8.7	16.2
Short-term external debt	−8.0	−2.0
Interest payments	3.4	1.3
Long-term external debt	3.0	1.2
Public and publicly guaranteed	3.0	1.2
IMF charges	0.3	0.0
Short-term external debt	0.1	0.0
Net transfers	5.2	15.0
Total external debt service paid	31.2	2.3
Other non-debt resource inflows		
Foreign direct investment	42.3	72.0
Portfolio equity	..	..
Major economic aggregates		
Gross national income (GNI)	1,974.4	2,008.8
Exports of goods, services and income	..	..
Workers' remittances & compensation of employees	..	..
Profit remittances on FDI	..	..
Ratios (%)		
External debt stocks to exports	..	..
External debt stocks to GNI	20	19
External debt service to exports	..	..
Present value of external debt to exports	..	76
Present value of external debt to GNI	..	12
Reserves to external debt stocks	53	47
Currency Composition (%)		
Euro	4.0	3.9
Japanese yen	0.0	0.0
U.S. dollar	61.2	68.3

Chad

Sub-Saharan Africa		Low income
Present value of external debt		1,845
Population (millions)		11.2
External debt per capita ($)		154.4
Share of public sector external debt in total (%)		98.6

	2009	2010
External debt stocks	1,746	1,733
Long-term external debt	1,714	1,708
Public and publicly guaranteed	1,714	1,708
Official creditors	1,682	1,679
Private creditors	32	30
Bonds	0	0
Private nonguaranteed	0	0
Use of International Monetary Fund (IMF) credit	29	17
Short-term external debt	4	8
Interest in arrears on long-term external debt	4	7
Disbursements	38	57
Long-term external debt	38	57
Public and publicly guaranteed	38	57
IMF purchases	0	0
Principal repayments	55	57
Long-term external debt	43	46
Public and publicly guaranteed	43	46
IMF repurchases	13	11
Net flows on external debt	–17	2
Short-term external debt	0	1
Interest payments	23	17
Long-term external debt	23	17
Public and publicly guaranteed	23	17
IMF charges	0	0
Short-term external debt	0	0
Net transfers	–41	–15
Total external debt service paid	78	73
Other non-debt resource inflows		
Foreign direct investment	462	781
Portfolio equity	..	..
Major economic aggregates		
Gross national income (GNI)	6,124	6,734
Exports of goods, services and income	..	..
Workers' remittances & compensation of employees	..	..
Profit remittances on FDI	..	..
Ratios (%)		
External debt stocks to exports	..	..
External debt stocks to GNI	29	26
External debt service to exports	..	..
Present value of external debt to exports	..	57
Present value of external debt to GNI	..	28
Reserves to external debt stocks	35	36
Currency Composition (%)		
Euro	3.3	3.2
Japanese yen	0.0	0.0
U.S. dollar	59.8	58.3

Chile

Latin America & Caribbean		Upper middle income
Present value of external debt		78,746
Population (millions)		17.1
External debt per capita ($)		5,045.6
Share of public sector external debt in total (%)		15.0

	2009	2010
External debt stocks	73,145	86,349
Long-term external debt	51,507	60,470
Public and publicly guaranteed	9,262	12,929
Official creditors	1,041	1,025
Private creditors	8,221	11,904
Bonds	5,413	8,413
Private nonguaranteed	42,245	47,541
Use of International Monetary Fund (IMF) credit	0	0
Short-term external debt	21,638	25,879
Interest in arrears on long-term external debt	0	0
Disbursements	19,343	19,677
Long-term external debt	19,343	19,677
Public and publicly guaranteed	2,385	4,010
IMF purchases	0	0
Principal repayments	15,574	11,005
Long-term external debt	15,574	11,005
Public and publicly guaranteed	1,903	336
IMF repurchases	0	0
Net flows on external debt	7,558	12,914
Short-term external debt	3,789	4,241
Interest payments	1,843	2,388
Long-term external debt	1,389	1,733
Public and publicly guaranteed	422	418
IMF charges	0	0
Short-term external debt	454	655
Net transfers	5,715	10,526
Total external debt service paid	17,417	13,392
Other non-debt resource inflows		
Foreign direct investment	12,874	15,095
Portfolio equity	328	1,748
Major economic aggregates		
Gross national income (GNI)	149,316	188,032
Exports of goods, services and income	67,984	87,820
Workers' remittances & compensation of employees	4	3
Profit remittances on FDI	14,801	18,956
Ratios (%)		
External debt stocks to exports	108	98
External debt stocks to GNI	49	46
External debt service to exports	26	15
Present value of external debt to exports	..	99
Present value of external debt to GNI	..	48
Reserves to external debt stocks	35	32
Currency Composition (%)		
Euro	1.0	0.7
Japanese yen	0.0	0.0
U.S. dollar	98.5	98.9

China

East Asia & Pacific	Upper middle income
Present value of external debt	522,861
Population (millions)	1,338.3
External debt per capita ($)	409.9
Share of public sector external debt in total (%)	16.4

	2009	2010
External debt stocks	432,197	548,551
Long-term external debt	191,688	201,027
Public and publicly guaranteed	94,038	90,180
Official creditors	68,358	67,204
Private creditors	25,681	22,976
Bonds	11,626	10,273
Private nonguaranteed	97,650	110,847
Use of International Monetary Fund (IMF) credit	0	0
Short-term external debt	240,509	347,524
Interest in arrears on long-term external debt	0	0
Disbursements	23,648	42,423
Long-term external debt	23,648	42,423
Public and publicly guaranteed	6,481	10,125
IMF purchases	0	0
Principal repayments	33,448	28,539
Long-term external debt	33,448	28,539
Public and publicly guaranteed	6,473	8,831
IMF repurchases	0	0
Net flows on external debt	43,521	120,899
Short-term external debt	53,321	107,015
Interest payments	6,330	34,071
Long-term external debt	3,122	6,269
Public and publicly guaranteed	2,108	2,626
IMF charges	0	0
Short-term external debt	3,208	27,802
Net transfers	37,190	86,827
Total external debt service paid	39,779	62,611
Other non-debt resource inflows		
Foreign direct investment	114,215	185,081
Portfolio equity	28,161	31,357
Major economic aggregates		
Gross national income (GNI)	5,034,545	5,906,327
Exports of goods, services and income	1,441,928	1,897,242
Workers' remittances & compensation of employees	48,729	51,300
Profit remittances on FDI	90,805	103,476
Ratios (%)		
External debt stocks to exports	30	29
External debt stocks to GNI	9	9
External debt service to exports	3	3
Present value of external debt to exports	..	31
Present value of external debt to GNI	..	10
Reserves to external debt stocks	568	531
Currency Composition (%)		
Euro	6.4	6.9
Japanese yen	7.8	7.3
U.S. dollar	83.7	84.0

Colombia

Latin America & Caribbean		Upper middle income
Present value of external debt		92,182
Population (millions)		46.3
External debt per capita ($)		1,362.2
Share of public sector external debt in total (%)		57.5

	2009	2010
External debt stocks	52,120	63,064
Long-term external debt	48,107	54,855
Public and publicly guaranteed	35,358	36,777
Official creditors	15,211	16,218
Private creditors	20,148	20,559
Bonds	17,159	17,686
Private nonguaranteed	12,749	18,078
Use of International Monetary Fund (IMF) credit	0	0
Short-term external debt	4,013	8,209
Interest in arrears on long-term external debt	0	0
Disbursements	13,146	12,840
Long-term external debt	13,146	12,840
Public and publicly guaranteed	8,105	3,499
IMF purchases	0	0
Principal repayments	5,914	6,553
Long-term external debt	5,914	6,553
Public and publicly guaranteed	1,789	2,306
IMF repurchases	0	0
Net flows on external debt	5,611	10,483
Short-term external debt	–1,620	4,196
Interest payments	2,912	3,227
Long-term external debt	2,723	2,842
Public and publicly guaranteed	2,005	2,135
IMF charges	0	0
Short-term external debt	189	386
Net transfers	2,700	7,255
Total external debt service paid	8,826	9,781
Other non-debt resource inflows		
Foreign direct investment	7,137	6,765
Portfolio equity	67	1,351
Major economic aggregates		
Gross national income (GNI)	226,344	276,093
Exports of goods, services and income	39,517	46,593
Workers' remittances & compensation of employees	4,180	4,058
Profit remittances on FDI	7,628	9,983
Ratios (%)		
External debt stocks to exports	132	135
External debt stocks to GNI	23	23
External debt service to exports	22	21
Present value of external debt to exports	..	212
Present value of external debt to GNI	..	38
Reserves to external debt stocks	48	45
Currency Composition (%)		
Euro	1.1	1.0
Japanese yen	2.2	2.3
U.S. dollar	94.3	94.9

Comoros

Sub-Saharan Africa		Low income
Present value of external debt		163
Population (thousands)		734.8
External debt per capita ($)		660.6
Share of public sector external debt in total (%)		96.7

	2009	2010
External debt stocks	277.6	485.4
Long-term external debt	263.4	469.3
Public and publicly guaranteed	263.4	469.3
Official creditors	263.4	469.3
Private creditors	0.0	0.0
Bonds	0.0	0.0
Private nonguaranteed	0.0	0.0
Use of International Monetary Fund (IMF) credit	10.1	12.3
Short-term external debt	4.0	3.8
Interest in arrears on long-term external debt	4.0	3.8
Disbursements	6.9	217.4
Long-term external debt	0.3	215.0
Public and publicly guaranteed	0.3	215.0
IMF purchases	6.5	2.4
Principal repayments	8.9	3.1
Long-term external debt	7.2	3.1
Public and publicly guaranteed	7.2	3.1
IMF repurchases	1.7	0.0
Net flows on external debt	−2.1	214.3
Short-term external debt	0.0	0.0
Interest payments	2.9	1.1
Long-term external debt	2.9	1.1
Public and publicly guaranteed	2.9	1.1
IMF charges	0.0	0.0
Short-term external debt	0.0	0.0
Net transfers	−5.0	213.1
Total external debt service paid	11.8	4.3
Other non-debt resource inflows		
Foreign direct investment	9.1	9.4
Portfolio equity	..	..
Major economic aggregates		
Gross national income (GNI)	534.6	538.8
Exports of goods, services and income	79.7	..
Workers' remittances & compensation of employees	..	..
Profit remittances on FDI	..	..
Ratios (%)		
External debt stocks to exports	348	..
External debt stocks to GNI	52	90
External debt service to exports	15	..
Present value of external debt to exports	..	240
Present value of external debt to GNI	..	31
Reserves to external debt stocks	54	30
Currency Composition (%)		
Euro	11.4	6.2
Japanese yen	0.0	0.0
U.S. dollar	43.8	69.9

Congo, Dem. Rep.

Sub-Saharan Africa	Low income
Present value of external debt	2,972
Population (millions)	66.0
External debt per capita ($)	87.5
Share of public sector external debt in total (%)	85.8

	2009	2010
External debt stocks	12,276	5,774
Long-term external debt	10,869	4,957
Public and publicly guaranteed	10,869	4,957
Official creditors	10,538	4,850
Private creditors	332	106
Bonds	0	0
Private nonguaranteed	0	0
Use of International Monetary Fund (IMF) credit	800	323
Short-term external debt	607	494
Interest in arrears on long-term external debt	493	280
Disbursements	387	116
Long-term external debt	105	40
Public and publicly guaranteed	105	40
IMF purchases	282	76
Principal repayments	376	140
Long-term external debt	226	83
Public and publicly guaranteed	226	83
IMF repurchases	150	57
Net flows on external debt	−81	76
Short-term external debt	−92	100
Interest payments	247	128
Long-term external debt	241	125
Public and publicly guaranteed	241	125
IMF charges	4	0
Short-term external debt	2	2
Net transfers	−328	−52
Total external debt service paid	623	268
Other non-debt resource inflows		
Foreign direct investment	664	2,939
Portfolio equity	..	..
Major economic aggregates		
Gross national income (GNI)	10,425	12,263
Exports of goods, services and income	5,047	7,125
Workers' remittances & compensation of employees	..	..
Profit remittances on FDI	..	..
Ratios (%)		
External debt stocks to exports	243	81
External debt stocks to GNI	118	47
External debt service to exports	12	4
Present value of external debt to exports	..	78
Present value of external debt to GNI	..	27
Reserves to external debt stocks	13	32
Currency Composition (%)		
Euro	29.2	7.3
Japanese yen	7.7	0.0
U.S. dollar	41.6	48.7

Congo, Rep.

Sub-Saharan Africa	Lower middle income
Present value of external debt	1,577
Population (millions)	4.0
External debt per capita ($)	935.1
Share of public sector external debt in total (%)	93.4

	2009	2010
External debt stocks	4,903	3,781
Long-term external debt	4,684	3,531
Public and publicly guaranteed	4,684	3,531
Official creditors	3,840	2,716
Private creditors	844	815
Bonds	0	0
Private nonguaranteed	0	0
Use of International Monetary Fund (IMF) credit	43	27
Short-term external debt	176	222
Interest in arrears on long-term external debt	107	105
Disbursements	10	75
Long-term external debt	7	73
Public and publicly guaranteed	7	73
IMF purchases	4	2
Principal repayments	86	151
Long-term external debt	86	151
Public and publicly guaranteed	86	151
IMF repurchases	0	0
Net flows on external debt	−144	−28
Short-term external debt	−68	48
Interest payments	77	45
Long-term external debt	75	42
Public and publicly guaranteed	75	42
IMF charges	0	0
Short-term external debt	2	3
Net transfers	−221	−72
Total external debt service paid	163	196
Other non-debt resource inflows		
Foreign direct investment	2,083	2,816
Portfolio equity	..	..
Major economic aggregates		
Gross national income (GNI)	6,878	8,619
Exports of goods, services and income	..	..
Workers' remittances & compensation of employees	15	15
Profit remittances on FDI	..	..
Ratios (%)		
External debt stocks to exports	..	..
External debt stocks to GNI	71	44
External debt service to exports	..	..
Present value of external debt to exports	..	19
Present value of external debt to GNI	..	20
Reserves to external debt stocks	78	118
Currency Composition (%)		
Euro	43.5	12.7
Japanese yen	0.0	0.0
U.S. dollar	43.6	78.9

Costa Rica

Latin America & Caribbean		Upper middle income
Present value of external debt		8,090
Population (millions)		4.7
External debt per capita ($)		1,899.3
Share of public sector external debt in total (%)		42.1

	2009	2010
External debt stocks	7,978	8,849
Long-term external debt	5,735	6,418
Public and publicly guaranteed	3,197	3,725
Official creditors	1,577	2,139
Private creditors	1,620	1,586
Bonds	1,435	1,435
Private nonguaranteed	2,538	2,693
Use of International Monetary Fund (IMF) credit	0	0
Short-term external debt	2,243	2,431
Interest in arrears on long-term external debt	0	0
Disbursements	1,322	1,504
Long-term external debt	1,322	1,504
Public and publicly guaranteed	523	770
IMF purchases	0	0
Principal repayments	795	653
Long-term external debt	795	653
Public and publicly guaranteed	500	266
IMF repurchases	0	0
Net flows on external debt	–1,218	1,038
Short-term external debt	–1,745	188
Interest payments	428	429
Long-term external debt	367	362
Public and publicly guaranteed	215	207
IMF charges	0	0
Short-term external debt	62	67
Net transfers	–1,646	609
Total external debt service paid	1,223	1,082
Other non-debt resource inflows		
Foreign direct investment	1,347	1,466
Portfolio equity	..	..
Major economic aggregates		
Gross national income (GNI)	28,767	33,001
Exports of goods, services and income	12,718	13,969
Workers' remittances & compensation of employees	513	552
Profit remittances on FDI	986	606
Ratios (%)		
External debt stocks to exports	63	63
External debt stocks to GNI	28	27
External debt service to exports	10	8
Present value of external debt to exports	..	59
Present value of external debt to GNI	..	27
Reserves to external debt stocks	51	52
Currency Composition (%)		
Euro	1.7	1.3
Japanese yen	5.1	5.9
U.S. dollar	87.9	89.1

Côte d'Ivoire

Sub-Saharan Africa	Lower middle income
Present value of external debt	10,597
Population (millions)	19.7
External debt per capita ($)	579.1
Share of public sector external debt in total (%)	91.1

	2009	2010
External debt stocks	11,702	11,430
Long-term external debt	11,251	10,696
Public and publicly guaranteed	10,980	10,416
Official creditors	8,914	8,673
Private creditors	2,066	1,743
Bonds	1,931	1,621
Private nonguaranteed	271	280
Use of International Monetary Fund (IMF) credit	352	383
Short-term external debt	99	351
Interest in arrears on long-term external debt	99	44
Disbursements	359	127
Long-term external debt	58	72
Public and publicly guaranteed	36	49
IMF purchases	301	55
Principal repayments	841	258
Long-term external debt	697	248
Public and publicly guaranteed	532	168
IMF repurchases	143	10
Net flows on external debt	−482	176
Short-term external debt	0	307
Interest payments	266	124
Long-term external debt	264	122
Public and publicly guaranteed	241	107
IMF charges	2	0
Short-term external debt	0	2
Net transfers	−748	51
Total external debt service paid	1,107	383
Other non-debt resource inflows		
Foreign direct investment	381	418
Portfolio equity	−9	..
Major economic aggregates		
Gross national income (GNI)	22,078	21,729
Exports of goods, services and income	11,702	..
Workers' remittances & compensation of employees	185	179
Profit remittances on FDI	..	..
Ratios (%)		
External debt stocks to exports	100	..
External debt stocks to GNI	53	53
External debt service to exports	9	..
Present value of external debt to exports	..	88
Present value of external debt to GNI	..	48
Reserves to external debt stocks	28	32
Currency Composition (%)		
Euro	58.6	57.6
Japanese yen	2.0	2.3
U.S. dollar	34.0	35.2

Djibouti

Middle East & North Africa		Lower middle income
Present value of external debt		500
Population (thousands)		888.7
External debt per capita ($)		845.4
Share of public sector external debt in total (%)		98.3

	2009	2010
External debt stocks	755.3	751.3
Long-term external debt	737.2	738.7
Public and publicly guaranteed	737.2	738.7
Official creditors	713.0	718.3
Private creditors	24.2	20.4
Bonds	0.0	0.0
Private nonguaranteed	0.0	0.0
Use of International Monetary Fund (IMF) credit	15.8	12.1
Short-term external debt	2.3	0.5
Interest in arrears on long-term external debt	2.3	0.5
Disbursements	69.6	37.3
Long-term external debt	67.4	37.3
Public and publicly guaranteed	67.4	37.3
IMF purchases	2.3	0.0
Principal repayments	26.7	25.7
Long-term external debt	22.5	22.4
Public and publicly guaranteed	22.5	22.4
IMF repurchases	4.2	3.3
Net flows on external debt	42.9	11.5
Short-term external debt	0.0	0.0
Interest payments	8.3	8.2
Long-term external debt	8.2	8.2
Public and publicly guaranteed	8.2	8.2
IMF charges	0.1	0.0
Short-term external debt	0.0	0.0
Net transfers	34.7	3.3
Total external debt service paid	35.0	33.9
Other non-debt resource inflows		
Foreign direct investment	96.9	26.8
Portfolio equity	0.0	0.0
Major economic aggregates		
Gross national income (GNI)	1,120.1	..
Exports of goods, services and income	436.4	453.6
Workers' remittances & compensation of employees	32.5	32.7
Profit remittances on FDI	6.5	0.0
Ratios (%)		
External debt stocks to exports	173	166
External debt stocks to GNI	67	..
External debt service to exports	8	7
Present value of external debt to exports	..	117
Present value of external debt to GNI	..	43
Reserves to external debt stocks	32	33
Currency Composition (%)		
Euro	30.5	28.3
Japanese yen	0.0	0.0
U.S. dollar	24.7	24.7

Dominica

Latin America & Caribbean	Upper middle income
Present value of external debt	202
Population (thousands)	67.8
External debt per capita ($)	3,935.4
Share of public sector external debt in total (%)	81.0

	2009	2010
External debt stocks	256.3	266.7
Long-term external debt	198.7	216.0
Public and publicly guaranteed	198.7	216.0
Official creditors	154.2	171.5
Private creditors	44.5	44.5
Bonds	40.3	40.3
Private nonguaranteed	0.0	0.0
Use of International Monetary Fund (IMF) credit	19.6	18.2
Short-term external debt	37.9	32.5
Interest in arrears on long-term external debt	17.9	1.5
Disbursements	13.4	29.4
Long-term external debt	8.3	29.4
Public and publicly guaranteed	8.3	29.4
IMF purchases	5.1	0.0
Principal repayments	15.7	11.1
Long-term external debt	14.9	10.0
Public and publicly guaranteed	14.9	10.0
IMF repurchases	0.8	1.1
Net flows on external debt	−48.3	29.4
Short-term external debt	−46.0	11.0
Interest payments	5.1	4.5
Long-term external debt	4.4	4.1
Public and publicly guaranteed	4.4	4.1
IMF charges	0.1	0.0
Short-term external debt	0.6	0.3
Net transfers	−53.4	24.9
Total external debt service paid	20.8	15.5
Other non-debt resource inflows		
Foreign direct investment	41.3	30.8
Portfolio equity	..	..
Major economic aggregates		
Gross national income (GNI)	359.8	364.4
Exports of goods, services and income	161.2	158.7
Workers' remittances & compensation of employees	25.4	26.2
Profit remittances on FDI	13.4	11.4
Ratios (%)		
External debt stocks to exports	159	168
External debt stocks to GNI	71	73
External debt service to exports	13	10
Present value of external debt to exports	..	124
Present value of external debt to GNI	..	56
Reserves to external debt stocks	29	29
Currency Composition (%)		
Euro	3.4	3.0
Japanese yen	0.0	0.0
U.S. dollar	85.1	80.6

Dominican Republic

Latin America & Caribbean		Upper middle income
Present value of external debt		10,906
Population (millions)		9.9
External debt per capita ($)		1,314.1
Share of public sector external debt in total (%)		69.8

	2009	2010
External debt stocks	11,046	13,045
Long-term external debt	8,600	9,958
Public and publicly guaranteed	7,757	9,115
Official creditors	5,327	6,165
Private creditors	2,431	2,950
Bonds	1,076	1,721
Private nonguaranteed	843	843
Use of International Monetary Fund (IMF) credit	767	1,139
Short-term external debt	1,679	1,948
Interest in arrears on long-term external debt	0	0
Disbursements	1,700	2,591
Long-term external debt	1,391	2,061
Public and publicly guaranteed	1,391	2,061
IMF purchases	308	530
Principal repayments	817	817
Long-term external debt	770	670
Public and publicly guaranteed	769	670
IMF repurchases	47	147
Net flows on external debt	627	2,044
Short-term external debt	−256	269
Interest payments	505	521
Long-term external debt	431	443
Public and publicly guaranteed	323	334
IMF charges	7	10
Short-term external debt	67	68
Net transfers	122	1,523
Total external debt service paid	1,322	1,337
Other non-debt resource inflows		
Foreign direct investment	2,067	1,626
Portfolio equity	..	..
Major economic aggregates		
Gross national income (GNI)	44,829	49,789
Exports of goods, services and income	10,918	12,171
Workers' remittances & compensation of employees	3,467	3,369
Profit remittances on FDI	1,577	0
Ratios (%)		
External debt stocks to exports	101	107
External debt stocks to GNI	25	26
External debt service to exports	12	11
Present value of external debt to exports	..	89
Present value of external debt to GNI	..	24
Reserves to external debt stocks	26	27
Currency Composition (%)		
Euro	8.6	6.4
Japanese yen	1.9	1.6
U.S. dollar	85.4	88.9

Ecuador

Latin America & Caribbean		Upper middle income
Present value of external debt		12,770
Population (millions)		14.5
External debt per capita ($)		1,024.2
Share of public sector external debt in total (%)		57.8

	2009	2010
External debt stocks	14,130	14,815
Long-term external debt	12,735	14,446
Public and publicly guaranteed	6,920	8,598
Official creditors	5,855	7,575
Private creditors	1,065	1,023
Bonds	873	868
Private nonguaranteed	5,815	5,848
Use of International Monetary Fund (IMF) credit	0	0
Short-term external debt	1,396	369
Interest in arrears on long-term external debt	37	37
Disbursements	1,419	3,059
Long-term external debt	1,419	3,059
Public and publicly guaranteed	384	2,307
IMF purchases	0	0
Principal repayments	4,388	1,351
Long-term external debt	4,388	1,351
Public and publicly guaranteed	3,526	633
IMF repurchases	0	0
Net flows on external debt	−3,264	681
Short-term external debt	−295	−1,027
Interest payments	642	498
Long-term external debt	578	484
Public and publicly guaranteed	329	325
IMF charges	0	0
Short-term external debt	64	14
Net transfers	−3,906	183
Total external debt service paid	5,030	1,849
Other non-debt resource inflows		
Foreign direct investment	316	167
Portfolio equity	2	..
Major economic aggregates		
Gross national income (GNI)	56,091	64,195
Exports of goods, services and income	15,607	19,686
Workers' remittances & compensation of employees	2,502	2,569
Profit remittances on FDI	822	..
Ratios (%)		
External debt stocks to exports	91	75
External debt stocks to GNI	25	23
External debt service to exports	32	9
Present value of external debt to exports	..	64
Present value of external debt to GNI	..	22
Reserves to external debt stocks	27	18
Currency Composition (%)		
Euro	4.1	2.8
Japanese yen	3.3	2.6
U.S. dollar	86.7	90.3

Egypt, Arab Rep.

Middle East & North Africa	Lower middle income
Present value of external debt	28,793
Population (millions)	81.1
External debt per capita ($)	429.5
Share of public sector external debt in total (%)	89.8

	2009	2010
External debt stocks	33,308	34,844
Long-term external debt	30,746	31,695
Public and publicly guaranteed	30,672	31,641
Official creditors	28,372	27,863
Private creditors	2,301	3,778
Bonds	1,883	3,333
Private nonguaranteed	74	54
Use of International Monetary Fund (IMF) credit	0	0
Short-term external debt	2,561	3,149
Interest in arrears on long-term external debt	0	0
Disbursements	2,071	3,382
Long-term external debt	2,071	3,382
Public and publicly guaranteed	2,062	3,377
IMF purchases	0	0
Principal repayments	2,040	2,106
Long-term external debt	2,040	2,106
Public and publicly guaranteed	2,021	2,080
IMF repurchases	0	0
Net flows on external debt	–250	1,864
Short-term external debt	–281	588
Interest payments	870	867
Long-term external debt	767	741
Public and publicly guaranteed	765	740
IMF charges	0	0
Short-term external debt	102	126
Net transfers	–1,120	997
Total external debt service paid	2,910	2,972
Other non-debt resource inflows		
Foreign direct investment	6,712	6,386
Portfolio equity	393	..
Major economic aggregates		
Gross national income (GNI)	189,138	214,548
Exports of goods, services and income	45,601	49,365
Workers' remittances & compensation of employees	7,150	7,725
Profit remittances on FDI	2,101	..
Ratios (%)		
External debt stocks to exports	73	71
External debt stocks to GNI	18	16
External debt service to exports	6	6
Present value of external debt to exports	..	46
Present value of external debt to GNI	..	15
Reserves to external debt stocks	105	106
Currency Composition (%)		
Euro	35.4	31.2
Japanese yen	12.7	13.1
U.S. dollar	34.1	38.3

El Salvador

Latin America & Caribbean		Lower middle income
Present value of external debt		9,732
Population (millions)		6.2
External debt per capita ($)		1,787.3
Share of public sector external debt in total (%)		57.7

	2009	2010
External debt stocks	10,102	11,069
Long-term external debt	9,239	9,964
Public and publicly guaranteed	6,100	6,394
Official creditors	3,836	4,175
Private creditors	2,264	2,220
Bonds	2,174	2,199
Private nonguaranteed	3,139	3,569
Use of International Monetary Fund (IMF) credit	0	0
Short-term external debt	863	1,105
Interest in arrears on long-term external debt	0	0
Disbursements	1,216	1,055
Long-term external debt	1,216	1,055
Public and publicly guaranteed	910	707
IMF purchases	0	0
Principal repayments	685	602
Long-term external debt	685	602
Public and publicly guaranteed	557	453
IMF repurchases	0	0
Net flows on external debt	−148	694
Short-term external debt	−679	242
Interest payments	491	477
Long-term external debt	475	464
Public and publicly guaranteed	373	349
IMF charges	0	0
Short-term external debt	15	13
Net transfers	−639	217
Total external debt service paid	1,175	1,080
Other non-debt resource inflows		
Foreign direct investment	231	−6
Portfolio equity	..	..
Major economic aggregates		
Gross national income (GNI)	20,437	20,815
Exports of goods, services and income	4,869	5,672
Workers' remittances & compensation of employees	3,405	3,449
Profit remittances on FDI	172	102
Ratios (%)		
External debt stocks to exports	207	195
External debt stocks to GNI	49	53
External debt service to exports	24	19
Present value of external debt to exports	..	177
Present value of external debt to GNI	..	46
Reserves to external debt stocks	31	26
Currency Composition (%)		
Euro	3.2	2.8
Japanese yen	5.2	5.2
U.S. dollar	85.3	86.5

Eritrea

Sub-Saharan Africa		Low income
Present value of external debt		597
Population (millions)		5.3
External debt per capita ($)		192.2
Share of public sector external debt in total (%)		99.3

	2009	2010
External debt stocks	1,019	1,010
Long-term external debt	1,013	1,003
Public and publicly guaranteed	1,013	1,003
Official creditors	972	965
Private creditors	41	38
Bonds	0	0
Private nonguaranteed	0	0
Use of International Monetary Fund (IMF) credit	0	0
Short-term external debt	6	7
Interest in arrears on long-term external debt	6	7
Disbursements	58	8
Long-term external debt	58	8
Public and publicly guaranteed	58	8
IMF purchases	0	0
Principal repayments	11	12
Long-term external debt	11	12
Public and publicly guaranteed	11	12
IMF repurchases	0	0
Net flows on external debt	46	–4
Short-term external debt	0	0
Interest payments	10	10
Long-term external debt	10	10
Public and publicly guaranteed	10	10
IMF charges	0	0
Short-term external debt	0	0
Net transfers	36	–14
Total external debt service paid	22	22
Other non-debt resource inflows		
Foreign direct investment	0	..
Portfolio equity	..	..
Major economic aggregates		
Gross national income (GNI)	1,839	2,097
Exports of goods, services and income	..	..
Workers' remittances & compensation of employees	..	..
Profit remittances on FDI	..	..
Ratios (%)		
External debt stocks to exports	..	..
External debt stocks to GNI	55	48
External debt service to exports	..	..
Present value of external debt to exports	..	732
Present value of external debt to GNI	..	34
Reserves to external debt stocks	9	11
Currency Composition (%)		
Euro	4.4	4.0
Japanese yen	0.0	0.0
U.S. dollar	67.8	67.4

Ethiopia

Sub-Saharan Africa		Low income
Present value of external debt		3,924
Population (millions)		82.9
External debt per capita ($)		86.2
Share of public sector external debt in total (%)		91.6

	2009	2010
External debt stocks	5,030	7,147
Long-term external debt	4,817	6,545
Public and publicly guaranteed	4,817	6,545
Official creditors	3,556	4,638
Private creditors	1,260	1,907
Bonds	0	0
Private nonguaranteed	0	0
Use of International Monetary Fund (IMF) credit	168	288
Short-term external debt	45	314
Interest in arrears on long-term external debt	32	30
Disbursements	2,310	1,882
Long-term external debt	2,145	1,760
Public and publicly guaranteed	2,145	1,760
IMF purchases	165	122
Principal repayments	62	130
Long-term external debt	62	130
Public and publicly guaranteed	62	130
IMF repurchases	0	0
Net flows on external debt	2,244	2,023
Short-term external debt	–5	271
Interest payments	42	62
Long-term external debt	40	50
Public and publicly guaranteed	40	50
IMF charges	0	0
Short-term external debt	1	13
Net transfers	2,203	1,961
Total external debt service paid	103	192
Other non-debt resource inflows		
Foreign direct investment	221	184
Portfolio equity	..	..
Major economic aggregates		
Gross national income (GNI)	31,921	29,625
Exports of goods, services and income	3,440	..
Workers' remittances & compensation of employees	262	225
Profit remittances on FDI	18	..
Ratios (%)		
External debt stocks to exports	146	..
External debt stocks to GNI	16	24
External debt service to exports	3	..
Present value of external debt to exports	..	107
Present value of external debt to GNI	..	13
Reserves to external debt stocks	35	..
Currency Composition (%)		
Euro	8.5	10.1
Japanese yen	0.0	0.0
U.S. dollar	68.8	70.3

Fiji

East Asia & Pacific		Lower middle income
Present value of external debt		403
Population (thousands)		860.6
External debt per capita ($)		525.4
Share of public sector external debt in total (%)		70.3

	2009	2010
External debt stocks	431.7	452.2
Long-term external debt	361.6	391.1
Public and publicly guaranteed	361.0	390.6
Official creditors	211.0	240.6
Private creditors	150.0	150.0
Bonds	150.0	150.0
Private nonguaranteed	0.5	0.5
Use of International Monetary Fund (IMF) credit	0.0	0.0
Short-term external debt	70.1	61.1
Interest in arrears on long-term external debt	0.1	0.1
Disbursements	15.2	32.6
Long-term external debt	15.2	32.6
Public and publicly guaranteed	15.0	32.6
IMF purchases	0.0	0.0
Principal repayments	9.8	7.6
Long-term external debt	9.8	7.6
Public and publicly guaranteed	9.7	7.6
IMF repurchases	0.0	0.0
Net flows on external debt	56.5	15.9
Short-term external debt	51.0	−9.0
Interest payments	15.0	14.2
Long-term external debt	14.4	13.3
Public and publicly guaranteed	14.4	13.3
IMF charges	0.0	0.0
Short-term external debt	0.6	0.9
Net transfers	41.5	1.8
Total external debt service paid	24.7	21.8
Other non-debt resource inflows		
Foreign direct investment	56.1	128.9
Portfolio equity	−1.1	..
Major economic aggregates		
Gross national income (GNI)	2,829.1	2,983.4
Exports of goods, services and income	1,393.5	..
Workers' remittances & compensation of employees	153.8	183.3
Profit remittances on FDI	30.3	..
Ratios (%)		
External debt stocks to exports	31	..
External debt stocks to GNI	15	15
External debt service to exports	2	..
Present value of external debt to exports	..	25
Present value of external debt to GNI	..	13
Reserves to external debt stocks	132	159
Currency Composition (%)		
Euro	0.6	0.5
Japanese yen	4.9	4.8
U.S. dollar	83.3	80.6

Gabon

Sub-Saharan Africa	Upper middle income
Present value of external debt	2,126
Population (millions)	1.5
External debt per capita ($)	1,548.5
Share of public sector external debt in total (%)	92.5

	2009	2010
External debt stocks	2,130	2,331
Long-term external debt	2,022	2,158
Public and publicly guaranteed	2,022	2,158
Official creditors	926	905
Private creditors	1,096	1,253
Bonds	901	879
Private nonguaranteed	0	0
Use of International Monetary Fund (IMF) credit	0	0
Short-term external debt	108	174
Interest in arrears on long-term external debt	5	6
Disbursements	260	482
Long-term external debt	260	482
Public and publicly guaranteed	260	482
IMF purchases	0	0
Principal repayments	315	307
Long-term external debt	315	307
Public and publicly guaranteed	315	307
IMF repurchases	0	0
Net flows on external debt	–60	240
Short-term external debt	–5	65
Interest payments	148	138
Long-term external debt	144	133
Public and publicly guaranteed	144	133
IMF charges	0	0
Short-term external debt	4	5
Net transfers	–208	102
Total external debt service paid	463	445
Other non-debt resource inflows		
Foreign direct investment	33	170
Portfolio equity	0	0
Major economic aggregates		
Gross national income (GNI)	9,874	11,467
Exports of goods, services and income	..	..
Workers' remittances & compensation of employees	..	..
Profit remittances on FDI	..	..
Ratios (%)		
External debt stocks to exports	..	..
External debt stocks to GNI	22	20
External debt service to exports	..	..
Present value of external debt to exports	..	16
Present value of external debt to GNI	..	19
Reserves to external debt stocks	94	74
Currency Composition (%)		
Euro	24.5	26.1
Japanese yen	0.2	0.2
U.S. dollar	55.1	54.7

Gambia, The

Sub-Saharan Africa		Low income
Present value of external debt		217
Population (millions)		1.7
External debt per capita ($)		272.0
Share of public sector external debt in total (%)		84.0

	2009	2010
External debt stocks	459.6	470.2
Long-term external debt	387.6	394.8
Public and publicly guaranteed	387.6	394.8
Official creditors	384.2	385.2
Private creditors	3.4	9.6
Bonds	0.0	0.0
Private nonguaranteed	0.0	0.0
Use of International Monetary Fund (IMF) credit	28.6	31.1
Short-term external debt	43.4	44.2
Interest in arrears on long-term external debt	2.4	2.2
Disbursements	49.3	46.9
Long-term external debt	33.5	43.9
Public and publicly guaranteed	33.5	43.9
IMF purchases	15.8	3.0
Principal repayments	11.3	12.5
Long-term external debt	11.3	12.5
Public and publicly guaranteed	11.3	12.5
IMF repurchases	0.0	0.0
Net flows on external debt	64.9	35.4
Short-term external debt	27.0	1.0
Interest payments	7.5	7.1
Long-term external debt	7.0	6.6
Public and publicly guaranteed	7.0	6.6
IMF charges	0.1	0.0
Short-term external debt	0.4	0.5
Net transfers	57.4	28.3
Total external debt service paid	18.8	19.6
Other non-debt resource inflows		
Foreign direct investment	39.4	37.4
Portfolio equity	..	..
Major economic aggregates		
Gross national income (GNI)	690.3	742.9
Exports of goods, services and income	290.0	270.0
Workers' remittances & compensation of employees	79.8	115.7
Profit remittances on FDI	11.7	11.5
Ratios (%)		
External debt stocks to exports	158	174
External debt stocks to GNI	67	63
External debt service to exports	6	7
Present value of external debt to exports	..	73
Present value of external debt to GNI	..	29
Reserves to external debt stocks	49	43
Currency Composition (%)		
Euro	5.0	5.9
Japanese yen	0.0	0.0
U.S. dollar	46.6	47.1

Georgia

Europe & Central Asia	Lower middle income
Present value of external debt	7,536
Population (millions)	4.5
External debt per capita ($)	2,074.6
Share of public sector external debt in total (%)	44.2

	2009	2010
External debt stocks	8,270	9,238
Long-term external debt	6,676	7,224
Public and publicly guaranteed	3,470	4,081
Official creditors	2,095	2,390
Private creditors	1,375	1,691
Bonds	500	750
Private nonguaranteed	3,207	3,143
Use of International Monetary Fund (IMF) credit	786	1,050
Short-term external debt	808	963
Interest in arrears on long-term external debt	7	7
Disbursements	1,488	1,487
Long-term external debt	1,147	1,190
Public and publicly guaranteed	678	815
IMF purchases	341	297
Principal repayments	502	532
Long-term external debt	474	510
Public and publicly guaranteed	140	169
IMF repurchases	28	22
Net flows on external debt	846	1,111
Short-term external debt	-140	156
Interest payments	280	281
Long-term external debt	248	245
Public and publicly guaranteed	74	84
IMF charges	7	12
Short-term external debt	25	25
Net transfers	565	830
Total external debt service paid	782	813
Other non-debt resource inflows		
Foreign direct investment	658	814
Portfolio equity	13	-20
Major economic aggregates		
Gross national income (GNI)	10,679	11,484
Exports of goods, services and income	3,630	4,480
Workers' remittances & compensation of employees	714	806
Profit remittances on FDI	263	471
Ratios (%)		
External debt stocks to exports	228	206
External debt stocks to GNI	77	80
External debt service to exports	22	18
Present value of external debt to exports	..	184
Present value of external debt to GNI	..	65
Reserves to external debt stocks	26	25
Currency Composition (%)		
Euro	8.0	8.1
Japanese yen	1.6	1.4
U.S. dollar	80.0	80.4

Ghana

Sub-Saharan Africa	Lower middle income
Present value of external debt	4,956
Population (millions)	24.4
External debt per capita ($)	343.1
Share of public sector external debt in total (%)	68.4

	2009	2010
External debt stocks	6,331	8,368
Long-term external debt	4,737	5,727
Public and publicly guaranteed	4,737	5,727
Official creditors	3,206	3,980
Private creditors	1,531	1,747
Bonds	750	750
Private nonguaranteed	0	0
Use of International Monetary Fund (IMF) credit	271	392
Short-term external debt	1,323	2,249
Interest in arrears on long-term external debt	41	13
Disbursements	1,022	1,280
Long-term external debt	918	1,155
Public and publicly guaranteed	918	1,155
IMF purchases	104	124
Principal repayments	101	120
Long-term external debt	101	120
Public and publicly guaranteed	101	120
IMF repurchases	0	0
Net flows on external debt	865	2,114
Short-term external debt	−56	954
Interest payments	131	200
Long-term external debt	99	144
Public and publicly guaranteed	99	144
IMF charges	1	0
Short-term external debt	31	56
Net transfers	734	1,914
Total external debt service paid	232	319
Other non-debt resource inflows		
Foreign direct investment	1,685	2,527
Portfolio equity	0	0
Major economic aggregates		
Gross national income (GNI)	25,871	30,776
Exports of goods, services and income	7,711	9,490
Workers' remittances & compensation of employees	114	136
Profit remittances on FDI	241	396
Ratios (%)		
External debt stocks to exports	82	88
External debt stocks to GNI	24	27
External debt service to exports	3	3
Present value of external debt to exports	..	61
Present value of external debt to GNI	..	18
Reserves to external debt stocks	..	..
Currency Composition (%)		
Euro	12.8	13.3
Japanese yen	0.0	0.0
U.S. dollar	60.6	60.1

Grenada

Latin America & Caribbean	Upper middle income
Present value of external debt	631
Population (thousands)	104.5
External debt per capita ($)	5,512.5
Share of public sector external debt in total (%)	85.9

	2009	2010
External debt stocks	558.6	576.0
Long-term external debt	497.2	494.8
Public and publicly guaranteed	497.2	494.8
Official creditors	277.3	279.2
Private creditors	219.9	215.6
Bonds	210.3	210.3
Private nonguaranteed	0.0	0.0
Use of International Monetary Fund (IMF) credit	23.0	29.1
Short-term external debt	38.3	52.1
Interest in arrears on long-term external debt	13.3	25.1
Disbursements	37.6	27.5
Long-term external debt	25.6	21.1
Public and publicly guaranteed	25.6	21.1
IMF purchases	12.0	6.4
Principal repayments	11.3	14.3
Long term external debt	9.1	14.3
Public and publicly guaranteed	9.1	14.3
IMF repurchases	2.3	0.0
Net flows on external debt	2.2	15.2
Short-term external debt	−24.0	2.0
Interest payments	11.7	11.2
Long-term external debt	11.1	10.9
Public and publicly guaranteed	11.1	10.9
IMF charges	0.1	0.0
Short-term external debt	0.5	0.3
Net transfers	−9.5	4.0
Total external debt service paid	23.0	25.5
Other non-debt resource inflows		
Foreign direct investment	102.6	63.6
Portfolio equity	..	..
Major economic aggregates		
Gross national income (GNI)	578.0	583.3
Exports of goods, services and income	183.8	178.0
Workers' remittances & compensation of employees	53.4	54.5
Profit remittances on FDI	55.4	35.4
Ratios (%)		
External debt stocks to exports	304	324
External debt stocks to GNI	97	99
External debt service to exports	13	14
Present value of external debt to exports	..	338
Present value of external debt to GNI	..	106
Reserves to external debt stocks	23	21
Currency Composition (%)		
Euro	0.3	0.3
Japanese yen	0.0	0.0
U.S. dollar	90.4	91.0

Guatemala

Latin America & Caribbean	Lower middle income
Present value of external debt	12,115
Population (millions)	14.4
External debt per capita ($)	996.6
Share of public sector external debt in total (%)	38.5

	2009	2010
External debt stocks	13,764	14,340
Long-term external debt	12,538	12,745
Public and publicly guaranteed	4,894	5,527
Official creditors	3,939	4,572
Private creditors	955	955
Bonds	955	955
Private nonguaranteed	7,644	7,218
Use of International Monetary Fund (IMF) credit	0	0
Short-term external debt	1,226	1,595
Interest in arrears on long-term external debt	0	0
Disbursements	934	1,442
Long-term external debt	934	1,442
Public and publicly guaranteed	807	879
IMF purchases	0	0
Principal repayments	1,019	913
Long-term external debt	1,019	913
Public and publicly guaranteed	268	263
IMF repurchases	0	0
Net flows on external debt	−1,010	898
Short-term external debt	−925	369
Interest payments	665	674
Long-term external debt	622	618
Public and publicly guaranteed	257	283
IMF charges	0	0
Short-term external debt	43	56
Net transfers	−1,675	224
Total external debt service paid	1,684	1,587
Other non-debt resource inflows		
Foreign direct investment	600	687
Portfolio equity	..	..
Major economic aggregates		
Gross national income (GNI)	36,569	39,990
Exports of goods, services and income	9,572	11,070
Workers' remittances & compensation of employees	4,019	4,229
Profit remittances on FDI	951	997
Ratios (%)		
External debt stocks to exports	144	130
External debt stocks to GNI	38	36
External debt service to exports	18	14
Present value of external debt to exports	..	118
Present value of external debt to GNI	..	32
Reserves to external debt stocks	38	41
Currency Composition (%)		
Euro	1.7	1.3
Japanese yen	3.5	3.8
U.S. dollar	90.1	91.2

Guinea

Sub-Saharan Africa		Low income
Present value of external debt		2,007
Population (millions)		10.0
External debt per capita ($)		292.8
Share of public sector external debt in total (%)		94.2

	2009	2010
External debt stocks	2,916	2,923
Long-term external debt	2,819	2,752
Public and publicly guaranteed	2,819	2,752
Official creditors	2,784	2,716
Private creditors	35	37
Bonds	0	0
Private nonguaranteed	0	0
Use of International Monetary Fund (IMF) credit	59	48
Short-term external debt	38	123
Interest in arrears on long-term external debt	36	55
Disbursements	49	36
Long-term external debt	49	36
Public and publicly guaranteed	49	36
IMF purchases	0	0
Principal repayments	95	63
Long-term external debt	82	53
Public and publicly guaranteed	82	53
IMF repurchases	13	10
Net flows on external debt	−200	39
Short-term external debt	−154	66
Interest payments	33	24
Long-term external debt	32	23
Public and publicly guaranteed	32	23
IMF charges	0	0
Short-term external debt	0	1
Net transfers	−232	15
Total external debt service paid	127	87
Other non-debt resource inflows		
Foreign direct investment	50	101
Portfolio equity	..	..
Major economic aggregates		
Gross national income (GNI)	3,692	4,231
Exports of goods, services and income	1,144	1,549
Workers' remittances & compensation of employees	64	60
Profit remittances on FDI	88	0
Ratios (%)		
External debt stocks to exports	255	189
External debt stocks to GNI	79	69
External debt service to exports	11	6
Present value of external debt to exports	..	145
Present value of external debt to GNI	..	54
Reserves to external debt stocks	..	..
Currency Composition (%)		
Euro	12.5	11.7
Japanese yen	1.7	1.7
U.S. dollar	65.3	65.4

Guinea-Bissau

Sub-Saharan Africa		Low income
Present value of external debt		124
Population (millions)		1.5
External debt per capita ($)		722.4
Share of public sector external debt in total (%)		88.0

	2009	2010
External debt stocks	1,118	1,095
Long-term external debt	950	963
Public and publicly guaranteed	950	963
Official creditors	950	963
Private creditors	0	0
Bonds	0	0
Private nonguaranteed	0	0
Use of International Monetary Fund (IMF) credit	10	4
Short-term external debt	158	128
Interest in arrears on long-term external debt	151	127
Disbursements	6	19
Long-term external debt	4	3
Public and publicly guaranteed	4	3
IMF purchases	3	16
Principal repayments	6	14
Long-term external debt	5	6
Public and publicly guaranteed	5	6
IMF repurchases	2	8
Net flows on external debt	5	−1
Short-term external debt	5	−6
Interest payments	4	3
Long-term external debt	4	3
Public and publicly guaranteed	4	3
IMF charges	0	0
Short-term external debt	0	0
Net transfers	1	−4
Total external debt service paid	10	17
Other non-debt resource inflows		
Foreign direct investment	14	9
Portfolio equity	..	..
Major economic aggregates		
Gross national income (GNI)	824	877
Exports of goods, services and income	..	..
Workers' remittances & compensation of employees	50	48
Profit remittances on FDI	..	..
Ratios (%)		
External debt stocks to exports	..	..
External debt stocks to GNI	136	125
External debt service to exports	..	..
Present value of external debt to exports	..	87
Present value of external debt to GNI	..	15
Reserves to external debt stocks	15	14
Currency Composition (%)		
Euro	11.6	9.5
Japanese yen	0.0	0.0
U.S. dollar	50.9	54.6

Guyana

Latin America & Caribbean	Lower middle income
Present value of external debt	762
Population (thousands)	754.5
External debt per capita ($)	1,794.0
Share of public sector external debt in total (%)	65.6

	2009	2010
External debt stocks	1,037	1,354
Long-term external debt	783	888
Public and publicly guaranteed	781	888
Official creditors	760	867
Private creditors	21	21
Bonds	0	0
Private nonguaranteed	2	0
Use of International Monetary Fund (IMF) credit	58	56
Short-term external debt	196	410
Interest in arrears on long-term external debt	97	103
Disbursements	105	124
Long-term external debt	105	124
Public and publicly guaranteed	105	124
IMF purchases	0	0
Principal repayments	8	17
Long-term external debt	8	16
Public and publicly guaranteed	8	16
IMF repurchases	0	1
Net flows on external debt	196	315
Short-term external debt	99	208
Interest payments	12	14
Long-term external debt	11	11
Public and publicly guaranteed	10	11
IMF charges	0	0
Short-term external debt	1	3
Net transfers	184	301
Total external debt service paid	20	31
Other non-debt resource inflows		
Foreign direct investment	144	188
Portfolio equity	..	..
Major economic aggregates		
Gross national income (GNI)	2,325	2,561
Exports of goods, services and income	..	..
Workers' remittances & compensation of employees	278	308
Profit remittances on FDI	..	..
Ratios (%)		
External debt stocks to exports	..	..
External debt stocks to GNI	45	53
External debt service to exports	..	..
Present value of external debt to exports	..	74
Present value of external debt to GNI	..	32
Reserves to external debt stocks	61	58
Currency Composition (%)		
Euro	2.9	2.2
Japanese yen	0.0	0.0
U.S. dollar	90.2	90.3

Haiti

Latin America & Caribbean		Low income
Present value of external debt		282
Population (millions)		10.0
External debt per capita ($)		49.2
Share of public sector external debt in total (%)		97.4

	2009	2010
External debt stocks	1,325.2	491.8
Long-term external debt	1,158.8	479.0
Public and publicly guaranteed	1,158.8	479.0
Official creditors	1,158.8	479.0
Private creditors	0.0	0.0
Bonds	0.0	0.0
Private nonguaranteed	0.0	0.0
Use of International Monetary Fund (IMF) credit	166.4	12.7
Short-term external debt	0.0	0.1
Interest in arrears on long-term external debt	0.0	0.1
Disbursements	272.5	410.9
Long-term external debt	212.0	286.1
Public and publicly guaranteed	212.0	286.1
IMF purchases	60.5	124.8
Principal repayments	29.6	122.5
Long-term external debt	26.5	122.5
Public and publicly guaranteed	26.5	122.5
IMF repurchases	3.1	0.0
Net flows on external debt	242.9	288.5
Short-term external debt	0.0	0.0
Interest payments	15.2	8.4
Long-term external debt	14.6	8.0
Public and publicly guaranteed	14.6	8.0
IMF charges	0.6	0.4
Short-term external debt	0.0	0.0
Net transfers	227.7	280.0
Total external debt service paid	44.7	130.9
Other non-debt resource inflows		
Foreign direct investment	38.0	150.0
Portfolio equity	..	..
Major economic aggregates		
Gross national income (GNI)	6,491.3	6,731.3
Exports of goods, services and income	963.9	836.2
Workers' remittances & compensation of employees	1,375.5	1,498.7
Profit remittances on FDI	..	..
Ratios (%)		
External debt stocks to exports	137	59
External debt stocks to GNI	20	7
External debt service to exports	5	16
Present value of external debt to exports	..	32
Present value of external debt to GNI	..	4
Reserves to external debt stocks	60	272
Currency Composition (%)		
Euro	4.1	9.2
Japanese yen	0.0	0.0
U.S. dollar	87.2	78.1

Honduras

Latin America & Caribbean	Lower middle income
Present value of external debt	1,971
Population (millions)	7.6
External debt per capita ($)	548.4
Share of public sector external debt in total (%)	67.1

	2009	2010
External debt stocks	3,674	4,168
Long-term external debt	3,325	3,740
Public and publicly guaranteed	2,445	2,798
Official creditors	2,358	2,714
Private creditors	87	84
Bonds	50	50
Private nonguaranteed	880	942
Use of International Monetary Fund (IMF) credit	32	30
Short-term external debt	317	398
Interest in arrears on long-term external debt	10	11
Disbursements	703	873
Long-term external debt	703	873
Public and publicly guaranteed	246	452
IMF purchases	0	0
Principal repayments	341	453
Long-term external debt	341	451
Public and publicly guaranteed	107	62
IMF repurchases	0	2
Net flows on external debt	155	500
Short-term external debt	−207	80
Interest payments	73	64
Long-term external debt	68	60
Public and publicly guaranteed	41	46
IMF charges	0	0
Short-term external debt	5	4
Net transfers	82	436
Total external debt service paid	414	517
Other non-debt resource inflows		
Foreign direct investment	523	797
Portfolio equity	..	..
Major economic aggregates		
Gross national income (GNI)	13,827	14,802
Exports of goods, services and income	5,852	6,818
Workers' remittances & compensation of employees	2,520	2,649
Profit remittances on FDI	499	567
Ratios (%)		
External debt stocks to exports	63	61
External debt stocks to GNI	27	28
External debt service to exports	7	8
Present value of external debt to exports	..	27
Present value of external debt to GNI	..	14
Reserves to external debt stocks	57	65
Currency Composition (%)		
Euro	10.0	8.3
Japanese yen	0.0	0.0
U.S. dollar	69.1	73.4

India

South Asia	Lower middle income
Present value of external debt	252,804
Population (millions)	1,170.9
External debt per capita ($)	247.9
Share of public sector external debt in total (%)	36.5

	2009	2010
External debt stocks	249,993	290,282
Long-term external debt	203,390	233,834
Public and publicly guaranteed	85,211	106,205
Official creditors	65,868	72,641
Private creditors	19,343	33,564
Bonds	9,521	20,430
Private nonguaranteed	118,180	127,629
Use of International Monetary Fund (IMF) credit	0	0
Short-term external debt	46,603	56,448
Interest in arrears on long-term external debt	0	0
Disbursements	26,631	43,420
Long-term external debt	26,631	43,420
Public and publicly guaranteed	10,380	24,351
IMF purchases	0	0
Principal repayments	10,985	14,708
Long-term external debt	10,985	14,708
Public and publicly guaranteed	5,331	5,190
IMF repurchases	0	0
Net flows on external debt	18,427	38,557
Short-term external debt	2,782	9,845
Interest payments	5,518	5,373
Long-term external debt	4,939	4,672
Public and publicly guaranteed	1,319	1,060
IMF charges	0	0
Short-term external debt	579	700
Net transfers	12,909	33,184
Total external debt service paid	16,503	20,081
Other non-debt resource inflows		
Foreign direct investment	35,596	24,159
Portfolio equity	21,112	39,972
Major economic aggregates		
Gross national income (GNI)	1,372,631	1,717,580
Exports of goods, services and income	274,989	358,876
Workers' remittances & compensation of employees	49,468	54,035
Profit remittances on FDI	12,278	13,385
Ratios (%)		
External debt stocks to exports	91	81
External debt stocks to GNI	18	17
External debt service to exports	6	6
Present value of external debt to exports	..	79
Present value of external debt to GNI	..	18
Reserves to external debt stocks	114	104
Currency Composition (%)		
Euro	4.9	3.7
Japanese yen	20.3	19.0
U.S. dollar	67.6	71.4

Indonesia

East Asia & Pacific	Lower middle income
Present value of external debt	159,754
Population (millions)	239.9
External debt per capita ($)	746.5
Share of public sector external debt in total (%)	50.8

	2009	2010
External debt stocks	162,850	179,064
Long-term external debt	138,801	147,809
Public and publicly guaranteed	85,967	91,024
Official creditors	63,270	66,484
Private creditors	22,696	24,540
Bonds	14,344	16,990
Private nonguaranteed	52,834	56,785
Use of International Monetary Fund (IMF) credit	0	0
Short-term external debt	24,050	31,255
Interest in arrears on long-term external debt	0	0
Disbursements	31,424	31,214
Long-term external debt	31,424	31,214
Public and publicly guaranteed	12,729	11,224
IMF purchases	0	0
Principal repayments	20,419	23,963
Long-term external debt	20,419	23,963
Public and publicly guaranteed	7,051	5,833
IMF repurchases	0	0
Net flows on external debt	14,566	14,456
Short-term external debt	3,561	7,205
Interest payments	4,459	5,335
Long-term external debt	4,301	4,944
Public and publicly guaranteed	2,802	3,034
IMF charges	0	0
Short-term external debt	159	391
Net transfers	10,107	9,121
Total external debt service paid	24,878	29,298
Other non-debt resource inflows		
Foreign direct investment	4,877	13,304
Portfolio equity	787	2,132
Major economic aggregates		
Gross national income (GNI)	520,467	686,633
Exports of goods, services and income	134,722	176,730
Workers' remittances & compensation of employees	6,793	6,916
Profit remittances on FDI	8,848	12,436
Ratios (%)		
External debt stocks to exports	121	101
External debt stocks to GNI	31	26
External debt service to exports	18	17
Present value of external debt to exports	..	102
Present value of external debt to GNI	..	28
Reserves to external debt stocks	41	54
Currency Composition (%)		
Euro	10.0	8.0
Japanese yen	32.4	34.7
U.S. dollar	51.8	51.8

Iran, Islamic Rep.

Middle East & North Africa		Upper middle income
Present value of external debt		10,954
Population (millions)		74.0
External debt per capita ($)		169.9
Share of public sector external debt in total (%)		50.9

	2009	2010
External debt stocks	13,464	12,570
Long-term external debt	7,553	6,411
Public and publicly guaranteed	7,553	6,411
Official creditors	2,272	2,025
Private creditors	5,280	4,385
Bonds	0	0
Private nonguaranteed	0	0
Use of International Monetary Fund (IMF) credit	0	0
Short-term external debt	5,911	6,159
Interest in arrears on long-term external debt	0	0
Disbursements	531	295
Long-term external debt	531	295
Public and publicly guaranteed	531	295
IMF purchases	0	0
Principal repayments	2,092	1,595
Long-term external debt	2,092	1,595
Public and publicly guaranteed	2,092	1,595
IMF repurchases	0	0
Net flows on external debt	−685	−1,052
Short-term external debt	876	248
Interest payments	485	371
Long-term external debt	278	139
Public and publicly guaranteed	278	139
IMF charges	0	0
Short-term external debt	207	232
Net transfers	−1,170	−1,423
Total external debt service paid	2,577	1,966
Other non-debt resource inflows		
Foreign direct investment	3,016	3,617
Portfolio equity	..	..
Major economic aggregates		
Gross national income (GNI)	328,593	..
Exports of goods, services and income	112,561	96,937
Workers' remittances & compensation of employees	1,072	1,181
Profit remittances on FDI	..	..
Ratios (%)		
External debt stocks to exports	..	..
External debt stocks to GNI	4	..
External debt service to exports	..	..
Present value of external debt to exports	..	..
Present value of external debt to GNI	..	3
Reserves to external debt stocks	..	..
Currency Composition (%)		
Euro	57.3	56.9
Japanese yen	7.4	7.5
U.S. dollar	32.7	33.1

Jamaica

Latin America & Caribbean		Upper middle income
Present value of external debt		13,246
Population (millions)		2.7
External debt per capita ($)		5,130.9
Share of public sector external debt in total (%)		54.8

	2009	2010
External debt stocks	10,987	13,865
Long-term external debt	9,943	11,900
Public and publicly guaranteed	6,702	7,593
Official creditors	2,406	3,259
Private creditors	4,296	4,334
Bonds	3,890	3,786
Private nonguaranteed	3,241	4,307
Use of International Monetary Fund (IMF) credit	0	785
Short-term external debt	1,044	1,180
Interest in arrears on long-term external debt	229	219
Disbursements	1,539	3,138
Long-term external debt	1,539	2,360
Public and publicly guaranteed	454	1,285
IMF purchases	0	778
Principal repayments	702	340
Long-term external debt	702	340
Public and publicly guaranteed	693	331
IMF repurchases	0	0
Net flows on external debt	656	2,944
Short-term external debt	–181	146
Interest payments	758	846
Long-term external debt	746	828
Public and publicly guaranteed	521	488
IMF charges	0	6
Short-term external debt	12	11
Net transfers	–101	2,098
Total external debt service paid	1,459	1,186
Other non-debt resource inflows		
Foreign direct investment	541	228
Portfolio equity	0	0
Major economic aggregates		
Gross national income (GNI)	12,018	13,305
Exports of goods, services and income	4,273	4,248
Workers' remittances & compensation of employees	1,912	2,011
Profit remittances on FDI	232	127
Ratios (%)		
External debt stocks to exports	257	326
External debt stocks to GNI	91	104
External debt service to exports	34	28
Present value of external debt to exports	..	221
Present value of external debt to GNI	..	102
Reserves to external debt stocks	19	18
Currency Composition (%)		
Euro	17.2	14.8
Japanese yen	2.6	2.5
U.S. dollar	76.3	79.6

Jordan

Middle East & North Africa	Upper middle income
Present value of external debt	6,672
Population (millions)	6.0
External debt per capita ($)	1,293.5
Share of public sector external debt in total (%)	81.4

	2009	2010
External debt stocks	6,615	7,822
Long-term external debt	5,445	6,504
Public and publicly guaranteed	5,445	6,504
Official creditors	5,101	5,420
Private creditors	344	1,084
Bonds	181	914
Private nonguaranteed	0	0
Use of International Monetary Fund (IMF) credit	12	8
Short-term external debt	1,158	1,310
Interest in arrears on long-term external debt	0	1
Disbursements	762	1,389
Long-term external debt	762	1,389
Public and publicly guaranteed	762	1,389
IMF purchases	0	0
Principal repayments	421	491
Long-term external debt	405	487
Public and publicly guaranteed	405	487
IMF repurchases	16	4
Net flows on external debt	73	1,049
Short-term external debt	−268	151
Interest payments	164	162
Long-term external debt	147	147
Public and publicly guaranteed	147	147
IMF charges	0	0
Short-term external debt	17	16
Net transfers	−91	887
Total external debt service paid	585	653
Other non-debt resource inflows		
Foreign direct investment	2,427	1,701
Portfolio equity	−30	−20
Major economic aggregates		
Gross national income (GNI)	25,696	28,081
Exports of goods, services and income	12,098	13,268
Workers' remittances & compensation of employees	3,597	3,641
Profit remittances on FDI	294	283
Ratios (%)		
External debt stocks to exports	55	59
External debt stocks to GNI	26	28
External debt service to exports	5	5
Present value of external debt to exports	..	51
Present value of external debt to GNI	..	26
Reserves to external debt stocks	183	174
Currency Composition (%)		
Euro	12.0	9.3
Japanese yen	25.9	22.6
U.S. dollar	31.1	37.1

Kazakhstan

Europe & Central Asia	Upper middle income
Present value of external debt	101,695
Population (millions)	16.3
External debt per capita ($)	7,276.4
Share of public sector external debt in total (%)	3.2

	2009	2010
External debt stocks	111,115	118,723
Long-term external debt	102,439	109,686
Public and publicly guaranteed	2,487	3,842
Official creditors	2,486	3,842
Private creditors	1	0
Bonds	0	0
Private nonguaranteed	99,952	105,844
Use of International Monetary Fund (IMF) credit	0	0
Short-term external debt	8,676	9,037
Interest in arrears on long-term external debt	0	0
Disbursements	30,524	50,133
Long-term external debt	30,524	50,133
Public and publicly guaranteed	717	1,519
IMF purchases	0	0
Principal repayments	20,103	42,789
Long-term external debt	20,103	42,789
Public and publicly guaranteed	131	278
IMF repurchases	0	0
Net flows on external debt	8,776	7,705
Short-term external debt	−1,645	361
Interest payments	5,677	4,971
Long-term external debt	5,373	4,655
Public and publicly guaranteed	58	54
IMF charges	0	0
Short-term external debt	304	316
Net transfers	3,099	2,734
Total external debt service paid	25,780	47,761
Other non-debt resource inflows		
Foreign direct investment	13,771	9,961
Portfolio equity	38	96
Major economic aggregates		
Gross national income (GNI)	102,471	125,913
Exports of goods, services and income	50,665	66,917
Workers' remittances & compensation of employees	261	291
Profit remittances on FDI	10,711	14,923
Ratios (%)		
External debt stocks to exports	219	177
External debt stocks to GNI	108	94
External debt service to exports	51	71
Present value of external debt to exports	..	155
Present value of external debt to GNI	..	89
Reserves to external debt stocks	21	24
Currency Composition (%)		
Euro	1.4	0.8
Japanese yen	40.1	24.5
U.S. dollar	55.9	73.2

Kenya

Sub-Saharan Africa		Low income
Present value of external debt		5,912
Population (millions)		40.5
External debt per capita ($)		207.4
Share of public sector external debt in total (%)		83.1

	2009	2010
External debt stocks	8,182	8,400
Long-term external debt	6,720	6,978
Public and publicly guaranteed	6,720	6,978
Official creditors	6,368	6,667
Private creditors	352	311
Bonds	0	0
Private nonguaranteed	0	0
Use of International Monetary Fund (IMF) credit	451	417
Short-term external debt	1,012	1,005
Interest in arrears on long-term external debt	73	80
Disbursements	747	530
Long-term external debt	538	530
Public and publicly guaranteed	538	530
IMF purchases	209	0
Principal repayments	275	284
Long-term external debt	257	258
Public and publicly guaranteed	257	258
IMF repurchases	18	26
Net flows on external debt	567	232
Short-term external debt	95	−14
Interest payments	111	115
Long-term external debt	85	90
Public and publicly guaranteed	85	90
IMF charges	2	0
Short-term external debt	23	25
Net transfers	456	117
Total external debt service paid	385	399
Other non-debt resource inflows		
Foreign direct investment	116	186
Portfolio equity	3	33
Major economic aggregates		
Gross national income (GNI)	29,311	31,264
Exports of goods, services and income	7,567	9,037
Workers' remittances & compensation of employees	1,686	1,777
Profit remittances on FDI	60	67
Ratios (%)		
External debt stocks to exports	108	93
External debt stocks to GNI	28	27
External debt service to exports	5	4
Present value of external debt to exports	..	72
Present value of external debt to GNI	..	20
Reserves to external debt stocks	47	51
Currency Composition (%)		
Euro	18.1	16.1
Japanese yen	17.9	18.4
U.S. dollar	45.3	43.7

KOSOVO

Europe & Central Asia		Lower middle income
Present value of external debt		241
Population (thousands)		1,815.0
External debt per capita ($)		188.6
Share of public sector external debt in total (%)		100.0

	2009	2010
External debt stocks	358.5	342.2
Long-term external debt	358.5	342.2
Public and publicly guaranteed	358.5	342.2
Official creditors	358.5	342.2
Private creditors	0.0	0.0
Bonds	0.0	0.0
Private nonguaranteed	0.0	0.0
Use of International Monetary Fund (IMF) credit	0.0	0.0
Short-term external debt	0.0	0.0
Interest in arrears on long-term external debt	0.0	0.0
Disbursements	0.0	0.0
Long-term external debt	0.0	0.0
Public and publicly guaranteed	0.0	0.0
IMF purchases	0.0	0.0
Principal repayments	207.7	16.3
Long-term external debt	207.7	16.3
Public and publicly guaranteed	207.7	16.3
IMF repurchases	0.0	0.0
Net flows on external debt	−207.7	−16.3
Short-term external debt	0.0	0.0
Interest payments	22.5	4.8
Long-term external debt	22.5	4.8
Public and publicly guaranteed	22.5	4.8
IMF charges	0.0	0.0
Short-term external debt	0.0	0.0
Net transfers	−230.3	−21.1
Total external debt service paid	230.3	21.1
Other non-debt resource inflows		
Foreign direct investment	408.1	413.4
Portfolio equity	0.0	0.0
Major economic aggregates		
Gross national income (GNI)	5,566.8	5,745.0
Exports of goods, services and income	1,100.8	1,343.1
Workers' remittances & compensation of employees	972.9	931.6
Profit remittances on FDI	102.0	38.2
Ratios (%)		
External debt stocks to exports	33	25
External debt stocks to GNI	6	6
External debt service to exports	21	2
Present value of external debt to exports	..	25
Present value of external debt to GNI	..	4
Reserves to external debt stocks	232	247
Currency Composition (%)		
Euro	0.0	0.0
Japanese yen	0.0	0.0
U.S. dollar	100.0	100.0

Kyrgyz Republic

Europe & Central Asia		Low income
Present value of external debt		1,750
Population (millions)		5.4
External debt per capita ($)		742.6
Share of public sector external debt in total (%)		61.3

	2009	2010
External debt stocks	3,986	3,984
Long-term external debt	3,395	3,612
Public and publicly guaranteed	2,320	2,442
Official creditors	2,320	2,442
Private creditors	0	0
Bonds	0	0
Private nonguaranteed	1,076	1,171
Use of International Monetary Fund (IMF) credit	167	177
Short-term external debt	424	195
Interest in arrears on long-term external debt	2	12
Disbursements	660	702
Long-term external debt	635	668
Public and publicly guaranteed	378	147
IMF purchases	26	34
Principal repayments	226	483
Long-term external debt	200	462
Public and publicly guaranteed	38	38
IMF repurchases	26	22
Net flows on external debt	472	−20
Short-term external debt	37	−238
Interest payments	43	73
Long-term external debt	37	69
Public and publicly guaranteed	19	23
IMF charges	1	0
Short-term external debt	5	4
Net transfers	429	−93
Total external debt service paid	268	557
Other non-debt resource inflows		
Foreign direct investment	189	438
Portfolio equity	1	−18
Major economic aggregates		
Gross national income (GNI)	4,500	4,466
Exports of goods, services and income	2,582	2,543
Workers' remittances & compensation of employees	992	1,275
Profit remittances on FDI	126	327
Ratios (%)		
External debt stocks to exports	154	157
External debt stocks to GNI	89	89
External debt service to exports	10	22
Present value of external debt to exports	..	66
Present value of external debt to GNI	..	38
Reserves to external debt stocks	40	43
Currency Composition (%)		
Euro	3.5	3.1
Japanese yen	13.0	14.0
U.S. dollar	69.2	68.9

Lao PDR

East Asia & Pacific	Lower middle income
Present value of external debt	3,959
Population (millions)	6.2
External debt per capita ($)	896.4
Share of public sector external debt in total (%)	52.9

	2009	2010
External debt stocks	5,458	5,559
Long-term external debt	5,442	5,549
Public and publicly guaranteed	2,818	2,939
Official creditors	2,818	2,939
Private creditors	0	0
Bonds	0	0
Private nonguaranteed	2,625	2,610
Use of International Monetary Fund (IMF) credit	16	10
Short-term external debt	0	0
Interest in arrears on long-term external debt	0	0
Disbursements	599	233
Long-term external debt	599	233
Public and publicly guaranteed	152	89
IMF purchases	0	0
Principal repayments	151	226
Long-term external debt	146	221
Public and publicly guaranteed	57	62
IMF repurchases	6	6
Net flows on external debt	447	6
Short-term external debt	0	0
Interest payments	69	79
Long-term external debt	69	79
Public and publicly guaranteed	25	29
IMF charges	0	0
Short-term external debt	0	0
Net transfers	379	–73
Total external debt service paid	220	305
Other non-debt resource inflows		
Foreign direct investment	319	350
Portfolio equity	0	0
Major economic aggregates		
Gross national income (GNI)	5,916	7,040
Exports of goods, services and income	1,486	..
Workers' remittances & compensation of employees	38	41
Profit remittances on FDI	43	..
Ratios (%)		
External debt stocks to exports	367	..
External debt stocks to GNI	92	79
External debt service to exports	15	..
Present value of external debt to exports	..	211
Present value of external debt to GNI	..	65
Reserves to external debt stocks	17	20
Currency Composition (%)		
Euro	0.0	0.0
Japanese yen	0.0	0.0
U.S. dollar	71.5	71.8

Latvia

Europe & Central Asia		Upper middle income
Present value of external debt		36,684
Population (millions)		2.2
External debt per capita ($)		17,635.7
Share of public sector external debt in total (%)		17.3

	2009	2010
External debt stocks	41,822	39,555
Long-term external debt	30,408	25,319
Public and publicly guaranteed	6,602	6,891
Official creditors	4,503	5,256
Private creditors	2,099	1,635
Bonds	1,152	1,069
Private nonguaranteed	23,806	18,428
Use of International Monetary Fund (IMF) credit	1,119	1,513
Short-term external debt	10,295	12,723
Interest in arrears on long-term external debt	0	0
Disbursements	10,372	7,103
Long-term external debt	10,097	6,694
Public and publicly guaranteed	4,504	1,237
IMF purchases	275	410
Principal repayments	6,628	9,671
Long-term external debt	6,628	9,671
Public and publicly guaranteed	47	478
IMF repurchases	0	0
Net flows on external debt	−105	−139
Short-term external debt	−3,849	2,428
Interest payments	946	876
Long-term external debt	772	686
Public and publicly guaranteed	111	178
IMF charges	17	33
Short-term external debt	156	156
Net transfers	−1,050	−1,015
Total external debt service paid	7,574	10,546
Other non-debt resource inflows		
Foreign direct investment	94	369
Portfolio equity	−8	9
Major economic aggregates		
Gross national income (GNI)	27,851	24,073
Exports of goods, services and income	12,555	13,808
Workers' remittances & compensation of employees	591	614
Profit remittances on FDI	−1,462	129
Ratios (%)		
External debt stocks to exports	333	286
External debt stocks to GNI	150	164
External debt service to exports	60	76
Present value of external debt to exports	..	260
Present value of external debt to GNI	..	129
Reserves to external debt stocks	17	19
Currency Composition (%)		
Euro	99.0	99.3
Japanese yen	0.0	0.0
U.S. dollar	1.0	0.7

Lebanon

Middle East & North Africa	Upper middle income
Present value of external debt	23,420
Population (millions)	4.2
External debt per capita ($)	5,746.3
Share of public sector external debt in total (%)	83.2

	2009	2010
External debt stocks	24,500	24,293
Long-term external debt	21,285	20,713
Public and publicly guaranteed	20,615	20,213
Official creditors	2,356	2,226
Private creditors	18,259	17,987
Bonds	17,704	17,422
Private nonguaranteed	670	500
Use of International Monetary Fund (IMF) credit	119	98
Short-term external debt	3,096	3,482
Interest in arrears on long-term external debt	0	0
Disbursements	3,332	2,143
Long-term external debt	3,332	2,143
Public and publicly guaranteed	3,132	2,143
IMF purchases	0	0
Principal repayments	3,096	2,651
Long-term external debt	3,096	2,632
Public and publicly guaranteed	3,096	2,462
IMF repurchases	0	19
Net flows on external debt	195	−122
Short-term external debt	−42	386
Interest payments	1,616	1,605
Long-term external debt	1,475	1,454
Public and publicly guaranteed	1,431	1,403
IMF charges	2	1
Short-term external debt	139	150
Net transfers	−1,421	−1,727
Total external debt service paid	4,711	4,256
Other non-debt resource inflows		
Foreign direct investment	4,804	4,955
Portfolio equity	929	−50
Major economic aggregates		
Gross national income (GNI)	34,194	40,032
Exports of goods, services and income	23,645	22,229
Workers' remittances & compensation of employees	7,558	5,114
Profit remittances on FDI	95	208
Ratios (%)		
External debt stocks to exports	104	109
External debt stocks to GNI	72	61
External debt service to exports	20	19
Present value of external debt to exports	..	98
Present value of external debt to GNI	..	67
Reserves to external debt stocks	160	183
Currency Composition (%)		
Euro	9.1	8.3
Japanese yen	0.3	0.4
U.S. dollar	86.9	87.9

Lesotho

Sub-Saharan Africa	Lower middle income
Present value of external debt	396
Population (millions)	2.2
External debt per capita ($)	334.3
Share of public sector external debt in total (%)	96.1

	2009	2010
External debt stocks	704.8	725.9
Long-term external debt	680.6	697.7
Public and publicly guaranteed	680.6	697.7
Official creditors	667.1	684.1
Private creditors	13.6	13.6
Bonds	0.0	0.0
Private nonguaranteed	0.0	0.0
Use of International Monetary Fund (IMF) credit	24.1	28.2
Short-term external debt	0.0	0.0
Interest in arrears on long-term external debt	0.0	0.0
Disbursements	37.4	52.7
Long-term external debt	37.4	40.8
Public and publicly guaranteed	37.4	40.8
IMF purchases	0.0	11.9
Principal repayments	30.6	27.1
Long-term external debt	24.6	19.6
Public and publicly guaranteed	24.6	19.6
IMF repurchases	5.9	7.5
Net flows on external debt	6.8	25.6
Short-term external debt	0.0	0.0
Interest payments	7.6	7.5
Long-term external debt	7.4	7.5
Public and publicly guaranteed	7.4	7.5
IMF charges	0.1	0.0
Short-term external debt	0.0	0.0
Net transfers	-0.8	18.2
Total external debt service paid	38.1	34.5
Other non-debt resource inflows		
Foreign direct investment	100.9	117.0
Portfolio equity	0.0	0.0
Major economic aggregates		
Gross national income (GNI)	2,267.8	2,552.8
Exports of goods, services and income	1,550.2	1,778.1
Workers' remittances & compensation of employees	623.0	745.9
Profit remittances on FDI	296.4	338.9
Ratios (%)		
External debt stocks to exports	45	41
External debt stocks to GNI	31	28
External debt service to exports	2	2
Present value of external debt to exports	..	24
Present value of external debt to GNI	..	17
Reserves to external debt stocks	..	..
Currency Composition (%)		
Euro	6.8	5.5
Japanese yen	0.0	0.0
U.S. dollar	43.6	45.3

Liberia

Sub-Saharan Africa		Low income
Present value of external debt		86
Population (millions)		4.0
External debt per capita ($)		57.1
Share of public sector external debt in total (%)		80.5

	2009	2010
External debt stocks	1,655.6	228.0
Long-term external debt	673.1	183.6
Public and publicly guaranteed	673.1	183.6
Official creditors	652.6	183.6
Private creditors	20.5	0.0
Bonds	0.0	0.0
Private nonguaranteed	0.0	0.0
Use of International Monetary Fund (IMF) credit	891.2	44.4
Short-term external debt	91.3	0.0
Interest in arrears on long-term external debt	91.3	0.0
Disbursements	17.6	17.3
Long-term external debt	0.0	3.7
Public and publicly guaranteed	0.0	3.7
IMF purchases	17.6	13.6
Principal repayments	36.3	3.7
Long-term external debt	36.3	3.7
Public and publicly guaranteed	36.3	3.7
IMF repurchases	0.0	0.0
Net flows on external debt	–18.6	13.5
Short-term external debt	0.0	0.0
Interest payments	27.7	1.8
Long-term external debt	16.8	0.6
Public and publicly guaranteed	16.8	0.6
IMF charges	10.9	1.2
Short-term external debt	0.0	0.0
Net transfers	–46.3	11.7
Total external debt service paid	64.0	5.5
Other non-debt resource inflows		
Foreign direct investment	217.8	452.9
Portfolio equity	..	..
Major economic aggregates		
Gross national income (GNI)	734.4	804.5
Exports of goods, services and income	472.2	430.9
Workers' remittances & compensation of employees	25.1	26.7
Profit remittances on FDI	5.8	0.1
Ratios (%)		
External debt stocks to exports	351	53
External debt stocks to GNI	225	28
External debt service to exports	14	1
Present value of external debt to exports	..	14
Present value of external debt to GNI	..	12
Reserves to external debt stocks	22	..
Currency Composition (%)		
Euro	2.6	0.0
Japanese yen	0.0	0.0
U.S. dollar	88.9	95.2

Lithuania

Europe & Central Asia	Upper middle income
Present value of external debt	27,225
Population (millions)	3.3
External debt per capita ($)	8,914.6
Share of public sector external debt in total (%)	39.4

	2009	2010
External debt stocks	31,821	29,602
Long-term external debt	25,871	24,133
Public and publicly guaranteed	9,072	11,664
Official creditors	1,251	1,612
Private creditors	7,820	10,053
Bonds	7,816	10,052
Private nonguaranteed	16,800	12,468
Use of International Monetary Fund (IMF) credit	0	0
Short-term external debt	5,949	5,469
Interest in arrears on long-term external debt	0	0
Disbursements	7,332	7,021
Long-term external debt	7,332	7,021
Public and publicly guaranteed	3,589	3,214
IMF purchases	0	0
Principal repayments	5,689	8,014
Long-term external debt	5,689	8,014
Public and publicly guaranteed	119	78
IMF repurchases	0	0
Net flows on external debt	−582	−1,473
Short-term external debt	−2,225	−480
Interest payments	765	807
Long-term external debt	586	669
Public and publicly guaranteed	273	506
IMF charges	0	0
Short-term external debt	178	138
Net transfers	−1,347	−2,280
Total external debt service paid	6,454	8,821
Other non-debt resource inflows		
Foreign direct investment	126	622
Portfolio equity	−2	37
Major economic aggregates		
Gross national income (GNI)	37,544	35,687
Exports of goods, services and income	20,948	25,745
Workers' remittances & compensation of employees	1,172	1,575
Profit remittances on FDI	−944	499
Ratios (%)		
External debt stocks to exports	152	115
External debt stocks to GNI	85	83
External debt service to exports	31	34
Present value of external debt to exports	..	107
Present value of external debt to GNI	..	69
Reserves to external debt stocks	21	23
Currency Composition (%)		
Euro	82.7	63.1
Japanese yen	0.0	0.0
U.S. dollar	17.2	36.9

Macedonia, FYR

Europe & Central Asia	Upper middle income
Present value of external debt	5,289
Population (millions)	2.1
External debt per capita ($)	2,816.8
Share of public sector external debt in total (%)	32.1

	2009	2010
External debt stocks	5,593	5,804
Long-term external debt	3,695	3,750
Public and publicly guaranteed	1,874	1,865
Official creditors	1,321	1,354
Private creditors	552	512
Bonds	468	434
Private nonguaranteed	1,821	1,885
Use of International Monetary Fund (IMF) credit	0	0
Short-term external debt	1,899	2,054
Interest in arrears on long-term external debt	30	59
Disbursements	1,012	576
Long-term external debt	1,012	576
Public and publicly guaranteed	347	182
IMF purchases	0	0
Principal repayments	375	455
Long-term external debt	375	455
Public and publicly guaranteed	88	98
IMF repurchases	0	0
Net flows on external debt	867	248
Short-term external debt	230	127
Interest payments	177	214
Long-term external debt	93	122
Public and publicly guaranteed	47	56
IMF charges	0	0
Short-term external debt	84	92
Net transfers	689	34
Total external debt service paid	552	669
Other non-debt resource inflows		
Foreign direct investment	197	296
Portfolio equity	−14	−4
Major economic aggregates		
Gross national income (GNI)	9,194	8,920
Exports of goods, services and income	3,726	4,402
Workers' remittances & compensation of employees	381	388
Profit remittances on FDI	138	239
Ratios (%)		
External debt stocks to exports	150	132
External debt stocks to GNI	61	65
External debt service to exports	15	15
Present value of external debt to exports	..	118
Present value of external debt to GNI	..	57
Reserves to external debt stocks	41	39
Currency Composition (%)		
Euro	69.6	69.6
Japanese yen	3.6	5.4
U.S. dollar	25.8	24.1

Madagascar

Sub-Saharan Africa		Low income
Present value of external debt		1,832
Population (millions)		20.7
External debt per capita ($)		110.8
Share of public sector external debt in total (%)		86.2

	2009	2010
External debt stocks	2,203	2,295
Long-term external debt	1,841	1,984
Public and publicly guaranteed	1,836	1,981
Official creditors	1,829	1,973
Private creditors	7	7
Bonds	0	0
Private nonguaranteed	4	3
Use of International Monetary Fund (IMF) credit	101	97
Short-term external debt	262	214
Interest in arrears on long-term external debt	189	188
Disbursements	126	211
Long-term external debt	126	211
Public and publicly guaranteed	124	211
IMF purchases	0	0
Principal repayments	34	39
Long-term external debt	34	37
Public and publicly guaranteed	32	36
IMF repurchases	0	2
Net flows on external debt	98	125
Short-term external debt	6	−47
Interest payments	17	17
Long-term external debt	15	16
Public and publicly guaranteed	15	16
IMF charges	0	0
Short-term external debt	1	1
Net transfers	82	109
Total external debt service paid	50	56
Other non-debt resource inflows		
Foreign direct investment	1,066	860
Portfolio equity	..	..
Major economic aggregates		
Gross national income (GNI)	8,397	8,628
Exports of goods, services and income	1,982	2,185
Workers' remittances & compensation of employees	..	..
Profit remittances on FDI	..	..
Ratios (%)		
External debt stocks to exports	111	105
External debt stocks to GNI	26	27
External debt service to exports	3	3
Present value of external debt to exports	..	60
Present value of external debt to GNI	..	21
Reserves to external debt stocks	52	51
Currency Composition (%)		
Euro	2.4	2.5
Japanese yen	0.0	0.0
U.S. dollar	52.5	53.1

Malawi

Sub-Saharan Africa		Low income
Present value of external debt		717
Population (millions)		14.9
External debt per capita ($)		61.8
Share of public sector external debt in total (%)		77.5

	2009	2010
External debt stocks	1033.3	921.6
Long-term external debt	839.4	714.6
Public and publicly guaranteed	839.4	714.6
Official creditors	833.6	714.6
Private creditors	5.8	0.0
Bonds	0.0	0.0
Private nonguaranteed	0.0	0.0
Use of International Monetary Fund (IMF) credit	126.9	146.0
Short-term external debt	67.0	61.0
Interest in arrears on long-term external debt	0.0	0.0
Disbursements	107.1	99.9
Long-term external debt	107.1	78.8
Public and publicly guaranteed	107.1	78.8
IMF purchases	0.0	21.2
Principal repayments	20.1	11.1
Long-term external debt	20.1	11.1
Public and publicly guaranteed	20.1	11.1
IMF repurchases	0.0	0.0
Net flows on external debt	154.0	82.9
Short-term external debt	67.0	−6.0
Interest payments	15.6	7.6
Long-term external debt	14.5	6.8
Public and publicly guaranteed	14.5	6.8
IMF charges	0.6	0.0
Short-term external debt	0.4	0.8
Net transfers	138.5	75.2
Total external debt service paid	35.7	18.7
Other non-debt resource inflows		
Foreign direct investment	60.0	140.0
Portfolio equity	..	..
Major economic aggregates		
Gross national income (GNI)	4,655.8	4,979.9
Exports of goods, services and income	..	..
Workers' remittances & compensation of employees	..	..
Profit remittances on FDI	..	..
Ratios (%)		
External debt stocks to exports	..	..
External debt stocks to GNI	22	19
External debt service to exports	..	..
Present value of external debt to exports	..	63
Present value of external debt to GNI	..	16
Reserves to external debt stocks	16	..
Currency Composition (%)		
Euro	3.2	2.6
Japanese yen	0.0	0.0
U.S. dollar	52.7	41.8

Malaysia

East Asia & Pacific		Upper middle income
Present value of external debt		75,406
Population (millions)		28.4
External debt per capita ($)		2,869.5
Share of public sector external debt in total (%)		26.1

	2009	2010
External debt stocks	66,272	81,497
Long-term external debt	42,578	46,421
Public and publicly guaranteed	21,245	25,795
Official creditors	4,092	3,750
Private creditors	17,154	22,045
Bonds	13,198	15,575
Private nonguaranteed	21,332	20,626
Use of International Monetary Fund (IMF) credit	0	0
Short-term external debt	23,695	35,076
Interest in arrears on long-term external debt	0	0
Disbursements	8,339	14,720
Long-term external debt	8,339	14,720
Public and publicly guaranteed	5,319	6,014
IMF purchases	0	0
Principal repayments	9,793	11,349
Long-term external debt	9,793	11,349
Public and publicly guaranteed	5,351	1,863
IMF repurchases	0	0
Net flows on external debt	−560	14,753
Short-term external debt	895	11,381
Interest payments	2,264	1,935
Long-term external debt	1,683	1,638
Public and publicly guaranteed	813	955
IMF charges	0	0
Short-term external debt	581	297
Net transfers	−2,824	12,818
Total external debt service paid	12,057	13,284
Other non-debt resource inflows		
Foreign direct investment	1,387	9,509
Portfolio equity	−449	..
Major economic aggregates		
Gross national income (GNI)	188,934	229,960
Exports of goods, services and income	197,637	254,129
Workers' remittances & compensation of employees	1,131	1,301
Profit remittances on FDI	11,119	..
Ratios (%)		
External debt stocks to exports	34	32
External debt stocks to GNI	35	35
External debt service to exports	6	5
Present value of external debt to exports	..	33
Present value of external debt to GNI	..	36
Reserves to external debt stocks	146	131
Currency Composition (%)		
Euro	0.1	0.1
Japanese yen	15.9	12.4
U.S. dollar	83.3	87.3

Maldives

South Asia	Upper middle income
Present value of external debt	1,020
Population (thousands)	315.9
External debt per capita ($)	3,889.1
Share of public sector external debt in total (%)	51.9

	2009	2010
External debt stocks	1,164	1,229
Long-term external debt	970	989
Public and publicly guaranteed	569	653
Official creditors	472	548
Private creditors	97	105
Bonds	0	0
Private nonguaranteed	400	336
Use of International Monetary Fund (IMF) credit	9	16
Short-term external debt	186	224
Interest in arrears on long-term external debt	1	3
Disbursements	199	212
Long-term external debt	191	204
Public and publicly guaranteed	114	143
IMF purchases	8	8
Principal repayments	150	179
Long-term external debt	147	179
Public and publicly guaranteed	47	53
IMF repurchases	3	1
Net flows on external debt	19	69
Short-term external debt	−30	36
Interest payments	26	24
Long-term external debt	21	14
Public and publicly guaranteed	13	10
IMF charges	0	0
Short-term external debt	6	10
Net transfers	−7	45
Total external debt service paid	176	203
Other non-debt resource inflows		
Foreign direct investment	112	164
Portfolio equity	..	..
Major economic aggregates		
Gross national income (GNI)	1,265	1,419
Exports of goods, services and income	834	953
Workers' remittances & compensation of employees	4	4
Profit remittances on FDI	26	31
Ratios (%)		
External debt stocks to exports	140	129
External debt stocks to GNI	92	87
External debt service to exports	21	21
Present value of external debt to exports	..	107
Present value of external debt to GNI	..	79
Reserves to external debt stocks	24	30
Currency Composition (%)		
Euro	18.7	18.3
Japanese yen	1.2	4.5
U.S. dollar	54.0	47.4

Mali

Sub-Saharan Africa		Low income
Present value of external debt		1,425
Population (millions)		15.4
External debt per capita ($)		151.4
Share of public sector external debt in total (%)		97.6

	2009	2010
External debt stocks	2,071	2,326
Long-term external debt	2,002	2,271
Public and publicly guaranteed	2,002	2,271
Official creditors	1,995	2,266
Private creditors	7	5
Bonds	0	0
Private nonguaranteed	0	0
Use of International Monetary Fund (IMF) credit	44	49
Short-term external debt	25	6
Interest in arrears on long-term external debt	1	0
Disbursements	497	318
Long-term external debt	494	312
Public and publicly guaranteed	494	312
IMF purchases	3	6
Principal repayments	46	39
Long-term external debt	46	39
Public and publicly guaranteed	46	39
IMF repurchases	0	0
Net flows on external debt	475	260
Short-term external debt	24	−18
Interest payments	22	22
Long-term external debt	22	21
Public and publicly guaranteed	22	21
IMF charges	0	0
Short-term external debt	0	0
Net transfers	453	239
Total external debt service paid	68	61
Other non-debt resource inflows		
Foreign direct investment	718	148
Portfolio equity	−3	..
Major economic aggregates		
Gross national income (GNI)	8,603	8,909
Exports of goods, services and income	2,180	2,425
Workers' remittances & compensation of employees	454	436
Profit remittances on FDI	430	0
Ratios (%)		
External debt stocks to exports	95	96
External debt stocks to GNI	24	26
External debt service to exports	3	3
Present value of external debt to exports	..	58
Present value of external debt to GNI	..	16
Reserves to external debt stocks	77	58
Currency Composition (%)		
Euro	3.1	3.5
Japanese yen	0.0	0.0
U.S. dollar	34.1	36.7

Mauritania

Sub-Saharan Africa	Lower middle income
Present value of external debt	2,364
Population (millions)	3.5
External debt per capita ($)	711.4
Share of public sector external debt in total (%)	88.3

	2009	2010
External debt stocks	2,048	2,461
Long-term external debt	1,840	2,174
Public and publicly guaranteed	1,840	2,174
Official creditors	1,827	2,173
Private creditors	12	1
Bonds	0	0
Private nonguaranteed	0	0
Use of International Monetary Fund (IMF) credit	16	50
Short-term external debt	192	237
Interest in arrears on long-term external debt	134	76
Disbursements	263	446
Long-term external debt	263	412
Public and publicly guaranteed	263	412
IMF purchases	0	34
Principal repayments	53	76
Long-term external debt	53	76
Public and publicly guaranteed	53	76
IMF repurchases	0	0
Net flows on external debt	102	473
Short-term external debt	−108	103
Interest payments	24	33
Long-term external debt	23	31
Public and publicly guaranteed	23	31
IMF charges	0	0
Short-term external debt	1	1
Net transfers	77	440
Total external debt service paid	78	109
Other non-debt resource inflows		
Foreign direct investment	−38	14
Portfolio equity	..	..
Major economic aggregates		
Gross national income (GNI)	3,079	3,672
Exports of goods, services and income	1,614	..
Workers' remittances & compensation of employees	..	..
Profit remittances on FDI	..	..
Ratios (%)		
External debt stocks to exports	127	..
External debt stocks to GNI	66	67
External debt service to exports	5	..
Present value of external debt to exports	..	126
Present value of external debt to GNI	..	68
Reserves to external debt stocks	12	12
Currency Composition (%)		
Euro	8.2	6.8
Japanese yen	0.0	0.0
U.S. dollar	38.9	44.3

Mauritius

Sub-Saharan Africa	Upper middle income
Present value of external debt	803
Population (millions)	1.3
External debt per capita ($)	839.6
Share of public sector external debt in total (%)	90.4

	2009	2010
External debt stocks	826	1,076
Long-term external debt	818	1,072
Public and publicly guaranteed	737	972
Official creditors	652	884
Private creditors	85	88
Bonds	0	0
Private nonguaranteed	81	100
Use of International Monetary Fund (IMF) credit	0	0
Short-term external debt	8	3
Interest in arrears on long-term external debt	0	0
Disbursements	285	388
Long-term external debt	285	388
Public and publicly guaranteed	217	319
IMF purchases	0	0
Principal repayments	108	113
Long-term external debt	108	113
Public and publicly guaranteed	71	64
IMF repurchases	0	0
Net flows on external debt	177	270
Short-term external debt	0	–4
Interest payments	21	17
Long-term external debt	20	17
Public and publicly guaranteed	20	16
IMF charges	0	0
Short-term external debt	1	0
Net transfers	156	253
Total external debt service paid	129	131
Other non-debt resource inflows		
Foreign direct investment	257	431
Portfolio equity	206	–40
Major economic aggregates		
Gross national income (GNI)	8,891	9,798
Exports of goods, services and income	4,635	5,413
Workers' remittances & compensation of employees	211	226
Profit remittances on FDI	195	92
Ratios (%)		
External debt stocks to exports	18	20
External debt stocks to GNI	9	11
External debt service to exports	3	2
Present value of external debt to exports	..	15
Present value of external debt to GNI	..	8
Reserves to external debt stocks	280	243
Currency Composition (%)		
Euro	40.8	32.0
Japanese yen	6.0	4.8
U.S. dollar	31.9	31.1

Mexico

Latin America & Caribbean	Upper middle income
Present value of external debt	178,631
Population (millions)	113.4
External debt per capita ($)	1,764.0
Share of public sector external debt in total (%)	55.7

	2009	2010
External debt stocks	171,485	200,081
Long-term external debt	143,895	161,068
Public and publicly guaranteed	99,374	111,467
Official creditors	21,212	25,655
Private creditors	78,161	85,813
Bonds	58,890	63,519
Private nonguaranteed	44,521	49,600
Use of International Monetary Fund (IMF) credit	0	0
Short-term external debt	27,590	39,013
Interest in arrears on long-term external debt	0	0
Disbursements	32,005	39,706
Long-term external debt	32,005	39,706
Public and publicly guaranteed	21,926	26,862
IMF purchases	0	0
Principal repayments	22,315	21,680
Long-term external debt	22,315	21,680
Public and publicly guaranteed	11,869	13,938
IMF repurchases	0	0
Net flows on external debt	8,875	29,449
Short-term external debt	−815	11,423
Interest payments	8,436	9,536
Long-term external debt	7,710	7,090
Public and publicly guaranteed	4,937	4,604
IMF charges	0	0
Short-term external debt	726	2,446
Net transfers	438	19,913
Total external debt service paid	30,751	31,216
Other non-debt resource inflows		
Foreign direct investment	15,334	18,679
Portfolio equity	4,169	641
Major economic aggregates		
Gross national income (GNI)	867,973	1,025,199
Exports of goods, services and income	249,740	319,198
Workers' remittances & compensation of employees	22,014	22,048
Profit remittances on FDI	7,891	6,576
Ratios (%)		
External debt stocks to exports	69	63
External debt stocks to GNI	20	20
External debt service to exports	12	10
Present value of external debt to exports	..	60
Present value of external debt to GNI	..	18
Reserves to external debt stocks	58	60
Currency Composition (%)		
Euro	7.4	6.4
Japanese yen	4.6	6.1
U.S. dollar	86.2	85.8

Moldova

Europe & Central Asia		Lower middle income
Present value of external debt		4,076
Population (millions)		3.6
External debt per capita ($)		1,295.6
Share of public sector external debt in total (%)		17.7

	2009	2010
External debt stocks	3,557	4,615
Long-term external debt	1,986	2,723
Public and publicly guaranteed	784	817
Official creditors	780	814
Private creditors	4	3
Bonds	0	0
Private nonguaranteed	1,203	1,906
Use of International Monetary Fund (IMF) credit	154	327
Short-term external debt	1,417	1,564
Interest in arrears on long-term external debt	38	37
Disbursements	271	642
Long-term external debt	271	459
Public and publicly guaranteed	41	89
IMF purchases	0	183
Principal repayments	316	307
Long-term external debt	301	299
Public and publicly guaranteed	53	48
IMF repurchases	15	8
Net flows on external debt	67	483
Short-term external debt	113	148
Interest payments	70	80
Long-term external debt	52	47
Public and publicly guaranteed	20	14
IMF charges	1	0
Short-term external debt	16	32
Net transfers	-2	404
Total external debt service paid	386	387
Other non-debt resource inflows		
Foreign direct investment	128	194
Portfolio equity	2	6
Major economic aggregates		
Gross national income (GNI)	5,743	6,280
Exports of goods, services and income	2,586	3,021
Workers' remittances & compensation of employees	1,211	1,370
Profit remittances on FDI	156	155
Ratios (%)		
External debt stocks to exports	138	153
External debt stocks to GNI	62	73
External debt service to exports	15	13
Present value of external debt to exports	..	136
Present value of external debt to GNI	..	65
Reserves to external debt stocks	42	37
Currency Composition (%)		
Euro	10.5	9.5
Japanese yen	3.0	2.9
U.S. dollar	66.6	69.4

Mongolia

East Asia & Pacific	Lower middle income
Present value of external debt	1,697
Population (millions)	2.8
External debt per capita ($)	886.8
Share of public sector external debt in total (%)	73.5

	2009	2010
External debt stocks	2,143	2,444
Long-term external debt	1,889	2,016
Public and publicly guaranteed	1,821	1,795
Official creditors	1,737	1,788
Private creditors	84	7
Bonds	75	0
Private nonguaranteed	68	221
Use of International Monetary Fund (IMF) credit	182	198
Short-term external debt	72	230
Interest in arrears on long-term external debt	0	0
Disbursements	411	270
Long-term external debt	246	246
Public and publicly guaranteed	219	76
IMF purchases	166	23
Principal repayments	79	144
Long-term external debt	73	139
Public and publicly guaranteed	64	121
IMF repurchases	7	5
Net flows on external debt	296	284
Short-term external debt	−36	158
Interest payments	31	28
Long-term external debt	29	24
Public and publicly guaranteed	26	20
IMF charges	1	2
Short-term external debt	1	2
Net transfers	265	256
Total external debt service paid	110	171
Other non-debt resource inflows		
Foreign direct investment	624	1,455
Portfolio equity	4	680
Major economic aggregates		
Gross national income (GNI)	4,388	5,522
Exports of goods, services and income	2,324	3,423
Workers' remittances & compensation of employees	200	277
Profit remittances on FDI	121	465
Ratios (%)		
External debt stocks to exports	92	71
External debt stocks to GNI	49	44
External debt service to exports	5	5
Present value of external debt to exports	..	58
Present value of external debt to GNI	..	33
Reserves to external debt stocks	62	94
Currency Composition (%)		
Euro	8.4	8.2
Japanese yen	20.3	22.6
U.S. dollar	43.7	39.9

Montenegro

Europe & Central Asia		Upper middle income
Present value of external debt		1,331
Population (thousands)		631.5
External debt per capita ($)		2,461.6
Share of public sector external debt in total (%)		86.8

	2009	2010
External debt stocks	2,315	1,554
Long-term external debt	1,108	1,368
Public and publicly guaranteed	1,093	1,350
Official creditors	893	837
Private creditors	201	512
Bonds	0	267
Private nonguaranteed	15	19
Use of International Monetary Fund (IMF) credit	0	0
Short-term external debt	1,207	186
Interest in arrears on long-term external debt	0	0
Disbursements	249	388
Long-term external debt	249	388
Public and publicly guaranteed	242	375
IMF purchases	0	0
Principal repayments	31	61
Long-term external debt	31	61
Public and publicly guaranteed	29	60
IMF repurchases	0	0
Net flows on external debt	823	−695
Short-term external debt	605	−1,021
Interest payments	40	38
Long-term external debt	28	34
Public and publicly guaranteed	28	33
IMF charges	0	0
Short-term external debt	12	4
Net transfers	783	−733
Total external debt service paid	71	99
Other non-debt resource inflows		
Foreign direct investment	1,527	760
Portfolio equity	−5	−8
Major economic aggregates		
Gross national income (GNI)	4,149	3,976
Exports of goods, services and income	1,583	1,681
Workers' remittances & compensation of employees	302	301
Profit remittances on FDI	90	100
Ratios (%)		
External debt stocks to exports	146	92
External debt stocks to GNI	56	39
External debt service to exports	4	6
Present value of external debt to exports	..	60
Present value of external debt to GNI	..	31
Reserves to external debt stocks	25	36
Currency Composition (%)		
Euro	59.8	69.1
Japanese yen	0.0	0.0
U.S. dollar	32.4	24.0

Morocco

Middle East & North Africa	Lower middle income
Present value of external debt	20,820
Population (millions)	32.0
External debt per capita ($)	795.1
Share of public sector external debt in total (%)	82.4

	2009	2010
External debt stocks	23,751	25,403
Long-term external debt	21,572	23,603
Public and publicly guaranteed	19,218	21,015
Official creditors	16,713	17,234
Private creditors	2,504	3,780
Bonds	0	1,336
Private nonguaranteed	2,354	2,589
Use of International Monetary Fund (IMF) credit	0	0
Short-term external debt	2,179	1,800
Interest in arrears on long-term external debt	0	0
Disbursements	4,551	4,970
Long-term external debt	4,551	4,970
Public and publicly guaranteed	3,468	3,854
IMF purchases	0	0
Principal repayments	2,709	2,436
Long-term external debt	2,709	2,436
Public and publicly guaranteed	1,138	1,282
IMF repurchases	0	0
Net flows on external debt	2,390	2,155
Short-term external debt	548	−379
Interest payments	702	875
Long-term external debt	678	850
Public and publicly guaranteed	612	819
IMF charges	0	0
Short-term external debt	24	26
Net transfers	1,688	1,279
Total external debt service paid	3,411	3,312
Other non-debt resource inflows		
Foreign direct investment	1,970	1,241
Portfolio equity	−4	132
Major economic aggregates		
Gross national income (GNI)	89,489	90,246
Exports of goods, services and income	27,306	30,997
Workers' remittances & compensation of employees	6,270	6,423
Profit remittances on FDI	1,753	1,445
Ratios (%)		
External debt stocks to exports	87	82
External debt stocks to GNI	27	28
External debt service to exports	12	11
Present value of external debt to exports	..	67
Present value of external debt to GNI	..	23
Reserves to external debt stocks	99	93
Currency Composition (%)		
Euro	54.5	55.4
Japanese yen	5.9	6.8
U.S. dollar	10.4	10.3

Mozambique

Sub-Saharan Africa		Low income
Present value of external debt		1,980
Population (millions)		23.4
External debt per capita ($)		176.3
Share of public sector external debt in total (%)		71.8

	2009	2010
External debt stocks	4,046	4,124
Long-term external debt	3,241	2,960
Public and publicly guaranteed	3,241	2,960
Official creditors	3,213	2,862
Private creditors	28	98
Bonds	0	0
Private nonguaranteed	0	0
Use of International Monetary Fund (IMF) credit	171	190
Short-term external debt	634	975
Interest in arrears on long-term external debt	467	878
Disbursements	605	378
Long-term external debt	452	356
Public and publicly guaranteed	452	356
IMF purchases	153	22
Principal repayments	15	40
Long-term external debt	15	40
Public and publicly guaranteed	15	40
IMF repurchases	0	0
Net flows on external debt	626	268
Short-term external debt	36	–70
Interest payments	29	50
Long-term external debt	23	47
Public and publicly guaranteed	23	47
IMF charges	0	0
Short-term external debt	5	3
Net transfers	598	218
Total external debt service paid	43	90
Other non-debt resource inflows		
Foreign direct investment	881	789
Portfolio equity	–0	0
Major economic aggregates		
Gross national income (GNI)	9,696	9,421
Exports of goods, services and income	2,629	3,052
Workers' remittances & compensation of employees	111	132
Profit remittances on FDI	84	70
Ratios (%)		
External debt stocks to exports	154	135
External debt stocks to GNI	42	44
External debt service to exports	2	3
Present value of external debt to exports	..	66
Present value of external debt to GNI	..	21
Reserves to external debt stocks	54	55
Currency Composition (%)		
Euro	6.8	9.5
Japanese yen	1.0	0.9
U.S. dollar	54.9	44.2

Myanmar

East Asia & Pacific		Low income
Present value of external debt		4,206
Population (millions)		48.0
External debt per capita ($)		132.4
Share of public sector external debt in total (%)		68.8

	2009	2010
External debt stocks	8,186	6,352
Long-term external debt	6,320	4,395
Public and publicly guaranteed	6,320	4,395
Official creditors	5,345	3,989
Private creditors	976	406
Bonds	0	0
Private nonguaranteed	0	0
Use of International Monetary Fund (IMF) credit	0	0
Short-term external debt	1,866	1,956
Interest in arrears on long-term external debt	1,009	1,116
Disbursements	0	1
Long-term external debt	0	1
Public and publicly guaranteed	0	1
IMF purchases	0	0
Principal repayments	9	651
Long-term external debt	9	651
Public and publicly guaranteed	9	651
IMF repurchases	0	0
Net flows on external debt	–83	–668
Short-term external debt	–74	–17
Interest payments	20	36
Long-term external debt	2	20
Public and publicly guaranteed	2	20
IMF charges	0	0
Short-term external debt	18	16
Net transfers	–103	–704
Total external debt service paid	29	687
Other non-debt resource inflows		
Foreign direct investment	323	756
Portfolio equity	..	..
Major economic aggregates		
Gross national income (GNI)	..	..
Exports of goods, services and income	..	..
Workers' remittances & compensation of employees	116	133
Profit remittances on FDI	..	..
Ratios (%)		
External debt stocks to exports	..	..
External debt stocks to GNI	..	..
External debt service to exports	..	..
Present value of external debt to exports	..	..
Present value of external debt to GNI	..	..
Reserves to external debt stocks	..	..
Currency Composition (%)		
Euro	10.3	13.1
Japanese yen	49.8	41.6
U.S. dollar	29.9	31.3

Nepal

South Asia	Low income
Present value of external debt	2,752
Population (millions)	30.0
External debt per capita ($)	123.6
Share of public sector external debt in total (%)	95.3

	2009	2010
External debt stocks	3,683	3,702
Long-term external debt	3,563	3,527
Public and publicly guaranteed	3,563	3,527
Official creditors	3,559	3,524
Private creditors	4	3
Bonds	0	0
Private nonguaranteed	0	0
Use of International Monetary Fund (IMF) credit	76	114
Short-term external debt	44	61
Interest in arrears on long-term external debt	0	0
Disbursements	127	177
Long-term external debt	127	134
Public and publicly guaranteed	127	134
IMF purchases	0	44
Principal repayments	143	154
Long-term external debt	140	149
Public and publicly guaranteed	140	149
IMF repurchases	2	4
Net flows on external debt	−29	41
Short-term external debt	−13	17
Interest payments	34	33
Long-term external debt	32	33
Public and publicly guaranteed	32	33
IMF charges	0	0
Short-term external debt	1	1
Net transfers	−63	7
Total external debt service paid	177	187
Other non-debt resource inflows		
Foreign direct investment	38	88
Portfolio equity	..	..
Major economic aggregates		
Gross national income (GNI)	13,050	15,823
Exports of goods, services and income	1,753	1,784
Workers' remittances & compensation of employees	2,986	3,468
Profit remittances on FDI	9	50
Ratios (%)		
External debt stocks to exports	210	208
External debt stocks to GNI	28	23
External debt service to exports	10	10
Present value of external debt to exports	..	151
Present value of external debt to GNI	..	20
Reserves to external debt stocks	..	..
Currency Composition (%)		
Euro	1.6	1.4
Japanese yen	7.1	7.3
U.S. dollar	42.3	41.9

Nicaragua

Latin America & Caribbean		Lower middle income
Present value of external debt		2,249
Population (millions)		5.8
External debt per capita ($)		826.9
Share of public sector external debt in total (%)		55.5

	2009	2010
External debt stocks	4,672	4,786
Long-term external debt	3,806	3,922
Public and publicly guaranteed	2,488	2,668
Official creditors	2,484	2,664
Private creditors	4	3
Bonds	0	0
Private nonguaranteed	1,318	1,255
Use of International Monetary Fund (IMF) credit	150	167
Short-term external debt	716	697
Interest in arrears on long-term external debt	484	495
Disbursements	803	583
Long-term external debt	766	563
Public and publicly guaranteed	291	267
IMF purchases	37	20
Principal repayments	386	415
Long-term external debt	386	415
Public and publicly guaranteed	61	55
IMF repurchases	0	0
Net flows on external debt	401	138
Short-term external debt	−15	−30
Interest payments	131	106
Long-term external debt	122	99
Public and publicly guaranteed	37	33
IMF charges	1	0
Short-term external debt	8	7
Net transfers	271	32
Total external debt service paid	517	521
Other non-debt resource inflows		
Foreign direct investment	434	508
Portfolio equity	..	..
Major economic aggregates		
Gross national income (GNI)	5,960	6,223
Exports of goods, services and income	2,891	3,637
Workers' remittances & compensation of employees	768	823
Profit remittances on FDI	121	135
Ratios (%)		
External debt stocks to exports	162	132
External debt stocks to GNI	78	77
External debt service to exports	18	14
Present value of external debt to exports	..	71
Present value of external debt to GNI	..	37
Reserves to external debt stocks	34	38
Currency Composition (%)		
Euro	4.7	5.1
Japanese yen	0.0	0.0
U.S. dollar	84.4	84.7

Niger

Sub-Saharan Africa	Low income
Present value of external debt	561
Population (millions)	15.5
External debt per capita ($)	72.6
Share of public sector external debt in total (%)	86.2

	2009	2010
External debt stocks	1,103	1,127
Long-term external debt	915	972
Public and publicly guaranteed	909	972
Official creditors	909	972
Private creditors	0	0
Bonds	0	0
Private nonguaranteed	7	0
Use of International Monetary Fund (IMF) credit	57	61
Short-term external debt	131	94
Interest in arrears on long-term external debt	17	26
Disbursements	108	95
Long-term external debt	103	90
Public and publicly guaranteed	103	90
IMF purchases	5	5
Principal repayments	36	18
Long-term external debt	36	18
Public and publicly guaranteed	29	11
IMF repurchases	0	0
Net flows on external debt	112	31
Short-term external debt	40	−46
Interest payments	10	9
Long-term external debt	8	8
Public and publicly guaranteed	8	8
IMF charges	0	0
Short-term external debt	1	1
Net transfers	103	22
Total external debt service paid	45	27
Other non-debt resource inflows		
Foreign direct investment	739	947
Portfolio equity	..	..
Major economic aggregates		
Gross national income (GNI)	5,204	5,493
Exports of goods, services and income	..	..
Workers' remittances & compensation of employees	94	88
Profit remittances on FDI	..	..
Ratios (%)		
External debt stocks to exports	..	..
External debt stocks to GNI	21	21
External debt service to exports	..	..
Present value of external debt to exports	..	53
Present value of external debt to GNI	..	10
Reserves to external debt stocks	59	67
Currency Composition (%)		
Euro	0.8	1.1
Japanese yen	0.0	0.0
U.S. dollar	46.1	47.3

Nigeria

Sub-Saharan Africa	Lower middle income
Present value of external debt	5,582
Population (millions)	158.4
External debt per capita ($)	49.8
Share of public sector external debt in total (%)	59.4

	2009	2010
External debt stocks	7,713	7,883
Long-term external debt	4,199	4,686
Public and publicly guaranteed	4,199	4,686
Official creditors	3,991	4,593
Private creditors	208	92
Bonds	0	0
Private nonguaranteed	0	0
Use of International Monetary Fund (IMF) credit	0	0
Short-term external debt	3,514	3,197
Interest in arrears on long-term external debt	0	0
Disbursements	519	1,051
Long-term external debt	519	1,051
Public and publicly guaranteed	519	1,051
IMF purchases	0	0
Principal repayments	339	246
Long-term external debt	339	246
Public and publicly guaranteed	339	246
IMF repurchases	0	0
Net flows on external debt	−3,762	488
Short-term external debt	−3,942	−317
Interest payments	153	103
Long-term external debt	84	59
Public and publicly guaranteed	84	59
IMF charges	0	0
Short-term external debt	69	44
Net transfers	−3,915	385
Total external debt service paid	492	349
Other non-debt resource inflows		
Foreign direct investment	8,555	6,049
Portfolio equity	487	2,161
Major economic aggregates		
Gross national income (GNI)	158,437	176,769
Exports of goods, services and income	59,274	77,756
Workers' remittances & compensation of employees	9,585	10,045
Profit remittances on FDI	15,042	19,121
Ratios (%)		
External debt stocks to exports	13	10
External debt stocks to GNI	5	4
External debt service to exports	1	0
Present value of external debt to exports	..	7
Present value of external debt to GNI	..	3
Reserves to external debt stocks	590	455
Currency Composition (%)		
Euro	4.8	3.9
Japanese yen	0.0	0.0
U.S. dollar	59.1	61.7

Pakistan

South Asia	Lower middle income
Present value of external debt	41,425
Population (millions)	173.6
External debt per capita ($)	327.0
Share of public sector external debt in total (%)	76.1

	2009	2010
External debt stocks	54,588	56,773
Long-term external debt	45,627	45,746
Public and publicly guaranteed	42,362	43,202
Official creditors	39,857	41,403
Private creditors	2,505	1,799
Bonds	2,150	1,550
Private nonguaranteed	3,265	2,544
Use of International Monetary Fund (IMF) credit	7,495	8,736
Short-term external debt	1,466	2,291
Interest in arrears on long-term external debt	0	0
Disbursements	7,728	3,646
Long-term external debt	4,413	2,012
Public and publicly guaranteed	3,732	1,857
IMF purchases	3,315	1,634
Principal repayments	2,472	3,273
Long-term external debt	2,241	3,008
Public and publicly guaranteed	1,635	2,132
IMF repurchases	231	265
Net flows on external debt	5,352	1,199
Short-term external debt	96	825
Interest payments	1,023	1,066
Long-term external debt	905	869
Public and publicly guaranteed	800	780
IMF charges	67	127
Short-term external debt	51	69
Net transfers	4,329	133
Total external debt service paid	3,495	4,338
Other non-debt resource inflows		
Foreign direct investment	2,338	2,016
Portfolio equity	−37	524
Major economic aggregates		
Gross national income (GNI)	166,370	181,599
Exports of goods, services and income	22,937	28,554
Workers' remittances & compensation of employees	8,717	9,690
Profit remittances on FDI	2,548	2,131
Ratios (%)		
External debt stocks to exports	238	199
External debt stocks to GNI	33	31
External debt service to exports	15	15
Present value of external debt to exports	..	159
Present value of external debt to GNI	..	24
Reserves to external debt stocks	25	30
Currency Composition (%)		
Euro	9.8	8.9
Japanese yen	16.9	18.8
U.S. dollar	46.2	44.6

Panama

Latin America & Caribbean	Upper middle income
Present value of external debt	10,049
Population (millions)	3.5
External debt per capita ($)	3,245.0
Share of public sector external debt in total (%)	91.3

	2009	2010
External debt stocks	11,267	11,412
Long-term external debt	11,267	11,412
Public and publicly guaranteed	10,131	10,421
Official creditors	1,833	2,127
Private creditors	8,298	8,293
Bonds	8,071	8,071
Private nonguaranteed	1,136	991
Use of International Monetary Fund (IMF) credit	0	0
Short-term external debt	0	0
Interest in arrears on long-term external debt	0	0
Disbursements	1,890	446
Long-term external debt	1,890	446
Public and publicly guaranteed	1,865	441
IMF purchases	0	0
Principal repayments	190	320
Long-term external debt	190	320
Public and publicly guaranteed	190	170
IMF repurchases	0	0
Net flows on external debt	1,700	126
Short-term external debt	0	0
Interest payments	716	757
Long-term external debt	716	757
Public and publicly guaranteed	628	670
IMF charges	0	0
Short-term external debt	0	0
Net transfers	984	−632
Total external debt service paid	906	1,077
Other non-debt resource inflows		
Foreign direct investment	1,773	2,363
Portfolio equity	..	..
Major economic aggregates		
Gross national income (GNI)	22,620	24,916
Exports of goods, services and income	18,157	18,948
Workers' remittances & compensation of employees	175	231
Profit remittances on FDI	1,397	1,815
Ratios (%)		
External debt stocks to exports	62	60
External debt stocks to GNI	50	46
External debt service to exports	5	6
Present value of external debt to exports	..	55
Present value of external debt to GNI	..	44
Reserves to external debt stocks	27	24
Currency Composition (%)		
Euro	0.0	0.0
Japanese yen	0.9	2.0
U.S. dollar	98.3	97.4

Papua New Guinea

East Asia & Pacific	Lower middle income
Present value of external debt	4,580
Population (millions)	6.9
External debt per capita ($)	848.9
Share of public sector external debt in total (%)	17.7

	2009	2010
External debt stocks	1,573	5,822
Long-term external debt	1,452	5,430
Public and publicly guaranteed	1,037	1,030
Official creditors	1,000	997
Private creditors	36	33
Bonds	0	0
Private nonguaranteed	415	4,400
Use of International Monetary Fund (IMF) credit	0	0
Short-term external debt	121	392
Interest in arrears on long-term external debt	0	0
Disbursements	516	3,153
Long-term external debt	516	3,153
Public and publicly guaranteed	33	37
IMF purchases	0	0
Principal repayments	514	759
Long-term external debt	514	759
Public and publicly guaranteed	63	68
IMF repurchases	0	0
Net flows on external debt	114	2,665
Short-term external debt	112	271
Interest payments	29	53
Long-term external debt	28	50
Public and publicly guaranteed	21	16
IMF charges	0	0
Short-term external debt	1	3
Net transfers	85	2,612
Total external debt service paid	543	812
Other non-debt resource inflows		
Foreign direct investment	423	30
Portfolio equity	..	..
Major economic aggregates		
Gross national income (GNI)	7,855	9,262
Exports of goods, services and income	4,626	6,278
Workers' remittances & compensation of employees	12	15
Profit remittances on FDI	537	..
Ratios (%)		
External debt stocks to exports	34	93
External debt stocks to GNI	20	63
External debt service to exports	12	13
Present value of external debt to exports	..	79
Present value of external debt to GNI	..	55
Reserves to external debt stocks	167	54
Currency Composition (%)		
Euro	4.3	3.8
Japanese yen	27.5	28.5
U.S. dollar	39.4	39.3

Paraguay

Latin America & Caribbean	Lower middle income
Present value of external debt	4,298
Population (millions)	6.5
External debt per capita ($)	765.0
Share of public sector external debt in total (%)	48.0

	2009	2010
External debt stocks	3,984	4,938
Long-term external debt	3,232	3,791
Public and publicly guaranteed	2,260	2,369
Official creditors	1,978	2,110
Private creditors	282	260
Bonds	0	0
Private nonguaranteed	972	1,421
Use of International Monetary Fund (IMF) credit	0	0
Short-term external debt	752	1,147
Interest in arrears on long-term external debt	0	0
Disbursements	489	826
Long-term external debt	489	826
Public and publicly guaranteed	248	303
IMF purchases	0	0
Principal repayments	308	320
Long-term external debt	308	320
Public and publicly guaranteed	262	246
IMF repurchases	0	0
Net flows on external debt	−213	901
Short-term external debt	−394	395
Interest payments	134	143
Long-term external debt	122	131
Public and publicly guaranteed	97	65
IMF charges	0	0
Short-term external debt	12	12
Net transfers	−347	757
Total external debt service paid	442	464
Other non-debt resource inflows		
Foreign direct investment	205	427
Portfolio equity	..	..
Major economic aggregates		
Gross national income (GNI)	13,954	19,497
Exports of goods, services and income	7,548	10,165
Workers' remittances & compensation of employees	609	673
Profit remittances on FDI	554	650
Ratios (%)		
External debt stocks to exports	53	49
External debt stocks to GNI	29	25
External debt service to exports	6	5
Present value of external debt to exports	..	48
Present value of external debt to GNI	..	26
Reserves to external debt stocks	97	84
Currency Composition (%)		
Euro	2.6	2.0
Japanese yen	19.3	19.3
U.S. dollar	67.5	70.2

Peru

Latin America & Caribbean		Upper middle income
Present value of external debt		32,384
Population (millions)		29.1
External debt per capita ($)		1,247.4
Share of public sector external debt in total (%)		53.9

	2009	2010
External debt stocks	36,393	36,271
Long-term external debt	31,662	30,216
Public and publicly guaranteed	20,800	20,027
Official creditors	11,740	10,573
Private creditors	9,061	9,454
Bonds	8,911	9,311
Private nonguaranteed	10,862	10,189
Use of International Monetary Fund (IMF) credit	0	0
Short-term external debt	4,731	6,055
Interest in arrears on long-term external debt	1	1
Disbursements	4,772	8,296
Long-term external debt	4,772	8,296
Public and publicly guaranteed	3,232	3,862
IMF purchases	0	0
Principal repayments	2,220	4,059
Long-term external debt	2,220	4,059
Public and publicly guaranteed	1,831	3,489
IMF repurchases	0	0
Net flows on external debt	1,883	5,561
Short-term external debt	−668	1,324
Interest payments	2,141	2,726
Long-term external debt	1,976	2,550
Public and publicly guaranteed	1,084	1,096
IMF charges	0	0
Short-term external debt	166	176
Net transfers	−258	2,835
Total external debt service paid	4,361	6,784
Other non-debt resource inflows		
Foreign direct investment	5,576	7,328
Portfolio equity	47	87
Major economic aggregates		
Gross national income (GNI)	122,566	147,315
Exports of goods, services and income	32,040	40,696
Workers' remittances & compensation of employees	2,409	2,534
Profit remittances on FDI	7,173	9,478
Ratios (%)		
External debt stocks to exports	114	89
External debt stocks to GNI	30	25
External debt service to exports	14	17
Present value of external debt to exports	..	89
Present value of external debt to GNI	..	25
Reserves to external debt stocks	91	122
Currency Composition (%)		
Euro	7.2	4.4
Japanese yen	12.1	9.9
U.S. dollar	77.8	83.5

Philippines

East Asia & Pacific	Lower middle income
Present value of external debt	62,514
Population (millions)	93.3
External debt per capita ($)	775.6
Share of public sector external debt in total (%)	61.6

	2009	2010
External debt stocks	63,116	72,337
Long-term external debt	59,114	66,042
Public and publicly guaranteed	41,944	44,641
Official creditors	22,067	23,198
Private creditors	19,877	21,443
Bonds	18,627	20,221
Private nonguaranteed	17,171	21,402
Use of International Monetary Fund (IMF) credit	0	0
Short-term external debt	4,002	6,295
Interest in arrears on long-term external debt	0	0
Disbursements	9,853	15,534
Long-term external debt	9,853	15,534
Public and publicly guaranteed	8,143	8,152
IMF purchases	0	0
Principal repayments	6,379	9,527
Long-term external debt	6,379	9,527
Public and publicly guaranteed	3,841	6,816
IMF repurchases	0	0
Net flows on external debt	476	8,300
Short-term external debt	−2,999	2,293
Interest payments	3,501	3,347
Long-term external debt	3,431	3,324
Public and publicly guaranteed	2,840	2,977
IMF charges	0	0
Short-term external debt	70	23
Net transfers	−3,025	4,953
Total external debt service paid	9,880	12,874
Other non-debt resource inflows		
Foreign direct investment	1,963	1,713
Portfolio equity	−1,096	481
Major economic aggregates		
Gross national income (GNI)	168,141	199,897
Exports of goods, services and income	54,336	70,020
Workers' remittances & compensation of employees	19,765	21,423
Profit remittances on FDI	2,150	2,234
Ratios (%)		
External debt stocks to exports	116	103
External debt stocks to GNI	38	36
External debt service to exports	18	18
Present value of external debt to exports	..	100
Present value of external debt to GNI	..	35
Reserves to external debt stocks	70	86
Currency Composition (%)		
Euro	5.1	3.6
Japanese yen	33.7	36.0
U.S. dollar	55.8	56.2

Romania

Europe & Central Asia		Upper middle income
Present value of external debt		101,112
Population (millions)		21.4
External debt per capita ($)		5,666.7
Share of public sector external debt in total (%)		16.4

	2009	2010
External debt stocks	118,008	121,505
Long-term external debt	86,253	81,383
Public and publicly guaranteed	17,956	20,557
Official creditors	11,271	14,233
Private creditors	6,686	6,324
Bonds	2,809	1,670
Private nonguaranteed	68,297	60,826
Use of International Monetary Fund (IMF) credit	9,544	15,092
Short-term external debt	22,210	25,029
Interest in arrears on long-term external debt	1	1
Disbursements	32,564	23,080
Long-term external debt	23,173	17,416
Public and publicly guaranteed	3,860	5,609
IMF purchases	9,391	5,664
Principal repayments	13,117	15,744
Long-term external debt	13,117	15,744
Public and publicly guaranteed	1,376	2,112
IMF repurchases	0	0
Net flows on external debt	12,998	10,155
Short-term external debt	−6,449	2,819
Interest payments	3,178	2,801
Long-term external debt	2,737	2,158
Public and publicly guaranteed	705	596
IMF charges	77	301
Short-term external debt	364	342
Net transfers	9,821	7,354
Total external debt service paid	16,295	18,545
Other non-debt resource inflows		
Foreign direct investment	4,846	3,453
Portfolio equity	7	4
Major economic aggregates		
Gross national income (GNI)	164,073	159,027
Exports of goods, services and income	52,162	59,372
Workers' remittances & compensation of employees	4,952	3,883
Profit remittances on FDI	1,212	747
Ratios (%)		
External debt stocks to exports	226	205
External debt stocks to GNI	72	76
External debt service to exports	31	31
Present value of external debt to exports	..	171
Present value of external debt to GNI	..	58
Reserves to external debt stocks	38	40
Currency Composition (%)		
Euro	78.8	82.5
Japanese yen	3.6	3.9
U.S. dollar	13.3	10.5

Russian Federation

Europe & Central Asia		Upper middle income
Present value of external debt		347,210
Population (millions)		141.8
External debt per capita ($)		2,714.2
Share of public sector external debt in total (%)		42.3

	2009	2010
External debt stocks	373,419	384,740
Long-term external debt	341,116	345,983
Public and publicly guaranteed	148,116	162,924
Official creditors	7,333	6,389
Private creditors	140,783	156,535
Bonds	70,117	82,643
Private nonguaranteed	193,000	183,059
Use of International Monetary Fund (IMF) credit	0	0
Short-term external debt	32,303	38,756
Interest in arrears on long-term external debt	427	56
Disbursements	42,090	51,406
Long-term external debt	42,090	51,406
Public and publicly guaranteed	32,106	33,633
IMF purchases	0	0
Principal repayments	38,944	44,197
Long-term external debt	38,944	44,197
Public and publicly guaranteed	15,841	19,153
IMF repurchases	0	0
Net flows on external debt	−19,124	14,034
Short-term external debt	−22,270	6,824
Interest payments	18,144	17,652
Long-term external debt	17,605	17,229
Public and publicly guaranteed	5,421	5,803
IMF charges	0	0
Short-term external debt	539	423
Net transfers	−37,268	−3,619
Total external debt service paid	57,088	61,849
Other non-debt resource inflows		
Foreign direct investment	36,500	42,868
Portfolio equity	3,369	−4,808
Major economic aggregates		
Gross national income (GNI)	1,181,785	1,431,459
Exports of goods, services and income	378,166	482,121
Workers' remittances & compensation of employees	5,359	5,264
Profit remittances on FDI	37,472	48,189
Ratios (%)		
External debt stocks to exports	99	80
External debt stocks to GNI	32	27
External debt service to exports	15	13
Present value of external debt to exports	..	72
Present value of external debt to GNI	..	25
Reserves to external debt stocks	118	125
Currency Composition (%)		
Euro	4.1	3.5
Japanese yen	0.5	0.4
U.S. dollar	93.5	94.5

Rwanda

Sub-Saharan Africa		Low income
Present value of external debt		595
Population (millions)		10.6
External debt per capita ($)		74.8
Share of public sector external debt in total (%)		96.3

	2009	2010
External debt stocks	748.9	794.6
Long-term external debt	723.5	765.6
Public and publicly guaranteed	723.5	765.6
Official creditors	723.5	765.6
Private creditors	0.0	0.0
Bonds	0.0	0.0
Private nonguaranteed	0.0	0.0
Use of International Monetary Fund (IMF) credit	15.2	14.9
Short-term external debt	10.1	14.1
Interest in arrears on long-term external debt	0.1	0.1
Disbursements	88.4	61.4
Long-term external debt	84.8	61.4
Public and publicly guaranteed	84.8	61.4
IMF purchases	3.6	0.0
Principal repayments	5.3	8.3
Long-term external debt	5.3	8.2
Public and publicly guaranteed	5.3	8.2
IMF repurchases	0.0	0.1
Net flows on external debt	88.1	57.0
Short-term external debt	5.0	4.0
Interest payments	6.0	6.2
Long-term external debt	5.8	6.0
Public and publicly guaranteed	5.8	6.0
IMF charges	0.1	0.0
Short-term external debt	0.1	0.2
Net transfers	82.1	50.9
Total external debt service paid	11.3	14.5
Other non-debt resource inflows		
Foreign direct investment	118.7	42.3
Portfolio equity	..	..
Major economic aggregates		
Gross national income (GNI)	5,225.2	5,581.8
Exports of goods, services and income	548.6	620.5
Workers' remittances & compensation of employees	92.6	91.8
Profit remittances on FDI	4.7	0.0
Ratios (%)		
External debt stocks to exports	137	128
External debt stocks to GNI	14	14
External debt service to exports	2	2
Present value of external debt to exports	..	103
Present value of external debt to GNI	..	12
Reserves to external debt stocks	99	102
Currency Composition (%)		
Euro	6.7	5.5
Japanese yen	0.0	0.0
U.S. dollar	41.2	40.1

Samoa

East Asia & Pacific		Lower middle income
Present value of external debt		174
Population (thousands)		183.1
External debt per capita ($)		1,682.4
Share of public sector external debt in total (%)		97.1

	2009	2010
External debt stocks	235.5	308.0
Long-term external debt	226.4	299.1
Public and publicly guaranteed	226.4	299.1
Official creditors	226.4	299.1
Private creditors	0.0	0.0
Bonds	0.0	0.0
Private nonguaranteed	0.0	0.0
Use of International Monetary Fund (IMF) credit	9.1	8.9
Short-term external debt	0.0	0.0
Interest in arrears on long-term external debt	0.0	0.0
Disbursements	34.1	78.9
Long-term external debt	25.2	78.9
Public and publicly guaranteed	25.2	78.9
IMF purchases	8.9	0.0
Principal repayments	6.0	7.2
Long-term external debt	6.0	7.2
Public and publicly guaranteed	6.0	7.2
IMF repurchases	0.0	0.0
Net flows on external debt	28.1	71.6
Short-term external debt	0.0	0.0
Interest payments	2.5	3.3
Long-term external debt	2.5	3.3
Public and publicly guaranteed	2.5	3.3
IMF charges	0.0	0.0
Short-term external debt	0.0	0.0
Net transfers	25.7	68.3
Total external debt service paid	8.5	10.6
Other non-debt resource inflows		
Foreign direct investment	9.9	0.7
Portfolio equity	..	..
Major economic aggregates		
Gross national income (GNI)	480.8	543.8
Exports of goods, services and income	181.5	201.7
Workers' remittances & compensation of employees	131.4	143.4
Profit remittances on FDI	27.4	17.5
Ratios (%)		
External debt stocks to exports	130	153
External debt stocks to GNI	49	57
External debt service to exports	5	5
Present value of external debt to exports	..	90
Present value of external debt to GNI	..	33
Reserves to external debt stocks	70	68
Currency Composition (%)		
Euro	0.8	0.4
Japanese yen	0.7	2.7
U.S. dollar	36.8	33.7

São Tomé and Príncipe

Sub-Saharan Africa	Lower middle income
Present value of external debt	49
Population (thousands)	165.4
External debt per capita ($)	1,028.8
Share of public sector external debt in total (%)	82.5

	2009	2010
External debt stocks	148.8	170.2
Long-term external debt	125.0	145.3
Public and publicly guaranteed	125.0	145.3
Official creditors	125.0	145.3
Private creditors	0.0	0.0
Bonds	0.0	0.0
Private nonguaranteed	0.0	0.0
Use of International Monetary Fund (IMF) credit	4.5	4.9
Short-term external debt	19.4	19.9
Interest in arrears on long-term external debt	8.4	5.9
Disbursements	19.4	20.3
Long-term external debt	18.8	19.8
Public and publicly guaranteed	18.8	19.8
IMF purchases	0.6	0.6
Principal repayments	1.7	1.2
Long-term external debt	1.7	1.2
Public and publicly guaranteed	1.7	1.2
IMF repurchases	0.0	0.0
Net flows on external debt	18.7	22.1
Short-term external debt	1.0	3.0
Interest payments	0.3	0.4
Long-term external debt	0.3	0.3
Public and publicly guaranteed	0.3	0.3
IMF charges	0.0	0.0
Short-term external debt	0.0	0.2
Net transfers	18.3	21.7
Total external debt service paid	2.1	1.6
Other non-debt resource inflows		
Foreign direct investment	7.5	3.0
Portfolio equity	..	..
Major economic aggregates		
Gross national income (GNI)	192.0	199.6
Exports of goods, services and income	21.3	24.7
Workers' remittances & compensation of employees	2.0	2.0
Profit remittances on FDI	..	..
Ratios (%)		
External debt stocks to exports	699	689
External debt stocks to GNI	78	85
External debt service to exports	10	7
Present value of external debt to exports	..	224
Present value of external debt to GNI	..	26
Reserves to external debt stocks	..	..
Currency Composition (%)		
Euro	3.8	14.9
Japanese yen	0.0	0.0
U.S. dollar	58.8	50.8

Senegal

Sub-Saharan Africa	Lower middle income
Present value of external debt	2,591
Population (millions)	12.4
External debt per capita ($)	295.7
Share of public sector external debt in total (%)	85.8

	2009	2010
External debt stocks	3,499	3,677
Long-term external debt	3,314	3,464
Public and publicly guaranteed	2,957	3,155
Official creditors	2,755	2,955
Private creditors	202	200
Bonds	200	200
Private nonguaranteed	357	308
Use of International Monetary Fund (IMF) credit	167	213
Short-term external debt	18	0
Interest in arrears on long-term external debt	0	0
Disbursements	935	485
Long-term external debt	835	436
Public and publicly guaranteed	627	353
IMF purchases	100	49
Principal repayments	148	227
Long-term external debt	148	227
Public and publicly guaranteed	98	82
IMF repurchases	0	1
Net flows on external debt	608	240
Short-term external debt	–179	–18
Interest payments	52	75
Long-term external debt	50	75
Public and publicly guaranteed	41	64
IMF charges	0	0
Short-term external debt	1	0
Net transfers	557	166
Total external debt service paid	200	302
Other non-debt resource inflows		
Foreign direct investment	208	237
Portfolio equity	..	..
Major economic aggregates		
Gross national income (GNI)	12,747	12,900
Exports of goods, services and income	..	..
Workers' remittances & compensation of employees	1,365	1,346
Profit remittances on FDI	..	..
Ratios (%)		
External debt stocks to exports	..	..
External debt stocks to GNI	27	29
External debt service to exports	..	..
Present value of external debt to exports	..	67
Present value of external debt to GNI	..	20
Reserves to external debt stocks	61	56
Currency Composition (%)		
Euro	17.7	18.8
Japanese yen	0.2	0.2
U.S. dollar	39.5	38.3

Serbia

Europe & Central Asia	Upper middle income
Present value of external debt	28,351
Population (millions)	7.3
External debt per capita ($)	4,418.4
Share of public sector external debt in total (%)	29.1

	2009	2010
External debt stocks	33,111	32,222
Long-term external debt	27,910	27,389
Public and publicly guaranteed	8,835	9,477
Official creditors	7,660	8,144
Private creditors	1,175	1,332
Bonds	0	0
Private nonguaranteed	19,076	17,912
Use of International Monetary Fund (IMF) credit	1,601	2,034
Short-term external debt	3,600	2,798
Interest in arrears on long-term external debt	712	352
Disbursements	6,104	5,052
Long-term external debt	4,529	4,594
Public and publicly guaranteed	966	1,365
IMF purchases	1,575	458
Principal repayments	3,613	3,431
Long-term external debt	3,613	3,431
Public and publicly guaranteed	158	351
IMF repurchases	0	0
Net flows on external debt	2,396	1,178
Short-term external debt	−95	−442
Interest payments	1,032	873
Long-term external debt	916	759
Public and publicly guaranteed	348	321
IMF charges	7	21
Short-term external debt	110	93
Net transfers	1,364	305
Total external debt service paid	4,644	4,305
Other non-debt resource inflows		
Foreign direct investment	1,936	1,340
Portfolio equity	22	84
Major economic aggregates		
Gross national income (GNI)	40,965	38,235
Exports of goods, services and income	12,544	13,933
Workers' remittances & compensation of employees	3,936	3,351
Profit remittances on FDI	451	552
Ratios (%)		
External debt stocks to exports	264	231
External debt stocks to GNI	81	84
External debt service to exports	37	31
Present value of external debt to exports	..	201
Present value of external debt to GNI	..	67
Reserves to external debt stocks	46	41
Currency Composition (%)		
Euro	42.4	46.6
Japanese yen	1.2	1.2
U.S. dollar	50.6	46.3

Seychelles

Sub-Saharan Africa **Upper middle income**

Present value of external debt		1,377
Population (thousands)		86.5
External debt per capita ($)		17,449.3
Share of public sector external debt in total (%)		33.0

	2009	2010
External debt stocks	1,723	1,510
Long-term external debt	736	498
Public and publicly guaranteed	736	498
Official creditors	300	248
Private creditors	436	250
Bonds	307	169
Private nonguaranteed	0	0
Use of International Monetary Fund (IMF) credit	19	31
Short-term external debt	968	980
Interest in arrears on long-term external debt	110	24
Disbursements	43	62
Long-term external debt	34	49
Public and publicly guaranteed	34	49
IMF purchases	9	13
Principal repayments	43	9
Long-term external debt	43	9
Public and publicly guaranteed	43	9
IMF repurchases	0	0
Net flows on external debt	93	151
Short-term external debt	94	98
Interest payments	18	40
Long-term external debt	8	28
Public and publicly guaranteed	8	28
IMF charges	0	0
Short-term external debt	10	12
Net transfers	75	111
Total external debt service paid	61	48
Other non-debt resource inflows		
Foreign direct investment	275	369
Portfolio equity	..	..
Major economic aggregates		
Gross national income (GNI)	702	855
Exports of goods, services and income	841	845
Workers' remittances & compensation of employees	12	11
Profit remittances on FDI	48	52
Ratios (%)		
External debt stocks to exports	205	179
External debt stocks to GNI	245	177
External debt service to exports	7	6
Present value of external debt to exports	..	155
Present value of external debt to GNI	..	173
Reserves to external debt stocks	11	16
Currency Composition (%)		
Euro	29.7	22.6
Japanese yen	1.0	0.0
U.S. dollar	55.4	60.4

Sierra Leone

Sub-Saharan Africa		Low income
Present value of external debt		432
Population (millions)		5.9
External debt per capita ($)		132.6
Share of public sector external debt in total (%)		84.9

	2009	2010
External debt stocks	701.0	778.0
Long-term external debt	604.8	660.9
Public and publicly guaranteed	604.8	660.9
Official creditors	393.7	449.8
Private creditors	211.1	211.1
Bonds	0.0	0.0
Private nonguaranteed	0.0	0.0
Use of International Monetary Fund (IMF) credit	73.2	113.0
Short-term external debt	23.0	4.1
Interest in arrears on long-term external debt	0.0	0.1
Disbursements	81.0	109.3
Long-term external debt	62.2	66.5
Public and publicly guaranteed	62.2	66.5
IMF purchases	18.8	42.8
Principal repayments	3.4	7.0
Long-term external debt	3.4	4.9
Public and publicly guaranteed	3.4	4.9
IMF repurchases	0.0	2.1
Net flows on external debt	91.6	83.3
Short-term external debt	14.0	−19.0
Interest payments	4.5	4.1
Long-term external debt	3.7	4.0
Public and publicly guaranteed	3.7	4.0
IMF charges	0.3	0.0
Short-term external debt	0.5	0.1
Net transfers	87.1	79.3
Total external debt service paid	7.9	11.1
Other non-debt resource inflows		
Foreign direct investment	74.3	86.6
Portfolio equity	5.6	..
Major economic aggregates		
Gross national income (GNI)	1,856.4	1,905.0
Exports of goods, services and income	339.8	432.6
Workers' remittances & compensation of employees	46.8	57.5
Profit remittances on FDI	39.0	46.2
Ratios (%)		
External debt stocks to exports	206	180
External debt stocks to GNI	38	41
External debt service to exports	2	3
Present value of external debt to exports	..	115
Present value of external debt to GNI	..	23
Reserves to external debt stocks	58	53
Currency Composition (%)		
Euro	3.2	2.4
Japanese yen	0.0	0.0
U.S. dollar	63.9	64.3

Solomon Islands

East Asia & Pacific	Lower middle income
Present value of external debt	148
Population (thousands)	538.1
External debt per capita ($)	400.4
Share of public sector external debt in total (%)	58.1

	2009	2010
External debt stocks	155.9	215.5
Long-term external debt	154.4	201.9
Public and publicly guaranteed	132.9	125.3
Official creditors	132.7	125.2
Private creditors	0.2	0.1
Bonds	0.0	0.0
Private nonguaranteed	21.5	76.6
Use of International Monetary Fund (IMF) credit	0.0	9.6
Short-term external debt	1.5	4.0
Interest in arrears on long-term external debt	1.5	4.0
Disbursements	13.7	46.4
Long-term external debt	13.7	36.8
Public and publicly guaranteed	−0.0	0.0
IMF purchases	0.0	9.5
Principal repayments	7.6	17.5
Long-term external debt	7.6	17.5
Public and publicly guaranteed	6.5	8.6
IMF repurchases	0.0	0.0
Net flows on external debt	6.1	28.9
Short-term external debt	0.0	0.0
Interest payments	2.4	3.2
Long-term external debt	2.4	3.2
Public and publicly guaranteed	1.8	1.7
IMF charges	0.0	0.0
Short-term external debt	0.0	0.0
Net transfers	3.7	25.7
Total external debt service paid	10.0	20.7
Other non-debt resource inflows		
Foreign direct investment	117.6	237.8
Portfolio equity	..	..
Major economic aggregates		
Gross national income (GNI)	473.1	554.7
Exports of goods, services and income	248.8	349.1
Workers' remittances & compensation of employees	2.4	2.9
Profit remittances on FDI	125.4	..
Ratios (%)		
External debt stocks to exports	63	62
External debt stocks to GNI	33	39
External debt service to exports	4	6
Present value of external debt to exports	..	47
Present value of external debt to GNI	..	28
Reserves to external debt stocks	94	123
Currency Composition (%)		
Euro	7.3	5.1
Japanese yen	0.0	0.0
U.S. dollar	77.7	79.2

Somalia

Sub-Saharan Africa		Low income
Present value of external debt		3,656
Population (millions)		9.3
External debt per capita ($)		315.3
Share of public sector external debt in total (%)		67.6

	2009	2010
External debt stocks	2,944	2,942
Long-term external debt	1,987	1,990
Public and publicly guaranteed	1,987	1,990
Official creditors	1,950	1,954
Private creditors	38	37
Bonds	0	0
Private nonguaranteed	0	0
Use of International Monetary Fund (IMF) credit	176	172
Short-term external debt	781	780
Interest in arrears on long-term external debt	781	780
Disbursements	0	0
Long-term external debt	0	0
Public and publicly guaranteed	0	0
IMF purchases	0	0
Principal repayments	0	0
Long-term external debt	0	0
Public and publicly guaranteed	0	0
IMF repurchases	0	0
Net flows on external debt	0	0
Short-term external debt	0	0
Interest payments	0	0
Long-term external debt	0	0
Public and publicly guaranteed	0	0
IMF charges	0	0
Short-term external debt	0	0
Net transfers	0	0
Total external debt service paid	0	0
Other non-debt resource inflows		
Foreign direct investment	108	112
Portfolio equity	..	..
Major economic aggregates		
Gross national income (GNI)	..	..
Exports of goods, services and income	..	..
Workers' remittances & compensation of employees	..	..
Profit remittances on FDI	..	..
Ratios (%)		
External debt stocks to exports	..	..
External debt stocks to GNI	..	..
External debt service to exports	..	..
Present value of external debt to exports	..	..
Present value of external debt to GNI	..	..
Reserves to external debt stocks	..	..
Currency Composition (%)		
Euro	6.5	6.0
Japanese yen	3.4	3.8
U.S. dollar	50.4	50.0

South Africa

Sub-Saharan Africa	Upper middle income
Present value of external debt	44,196
Population (millions)	50.0
External debt per capita ($)	903.5
Share of public sector external debt in total (%)	39.3

	2009	2010
External debt stocks	42,466	45,165
Long-term external debt	29,192	32,860
Public and publicly guaranteed	15,428	17,753
Official creditors	227	1,139
Private creditors	15,201	16,614
Bonds	9,279	11,065
Private nonguaranteed	13,764	15,107
Use of International Monetary Fund (IMF) credit	0	0
Short-term external debt	13,274	12,305
Interest in arrears on long-term external debt	0	0
Disbursements	4,339	5,698
Long-term external debt	4,339	5,698
Public and publicly guaranteed	2,332	3,777
IMF purchases	0	0
Principal repayments	2,127	2,608
Long-term external debt	2,127	2,608
Public and publicly guaranteed	1,419	1,278
IMF repurchases	0	0
Net flows on external debt	−2,451	2,121
Short-term external debt	−4,663	−969
Interest payments	1,615	2,476
Long-term external debt	1,146	2,092
Public and publicly guaranteed	686	716
IMF charges	0	0
Short-term external debt	468	384
Net transfers	−4,065	−355
Total external debt service paid	3,741	5,084
Other non-debt resource inflows		
Foreign direct investment	5,354	1,565
Portfolio equity	9,364	5,826
Major economic aggregates		
Gross national income (GNI)	276,439	356,475
Exports of goods, services and income	82,551	104,355
Workers' remittances & compensation of employees	902	1,119
Profit remittances on FDI	5,279	6,165
Ratios (%)		
External debt stocks to exports	51	43
External debt stocks to GNI	15	13
External debt service to exports	5	5
Present value of external debt to exports	..	45
Present value of external debt to GNI	..	15
Reserves to external debt stocks	93	97
Currency Composition (%)		
Euro	19.1	15.4
Japanese yen	0.0	0.0
U.S. dollar	79.6	80.4

Sri Lanka

South Asia		Lower middle income
Present value of external debt		15,887
Population (millions)		20.9
External debt per capita ($)		980.5
Share of public sector external debt in total (%)		80.4

	2009	2010
External debt stocks	17,213	20,452
Long-term external debt	14,618	17,368
Public and publicly guaranteed	13,652	16,449
Official creditors	11,934	13,602
Private creditors	1,718	2,847
Bonds	1,000	2,000
Private nonguaranteed	967	919
Use of International Monetary Fund (IMF) credit	721	1,311
Short-term external debt	1,873	1,773
Interest in arrears on long-term external debt	24	28
Disbursements	2,846	3,715
Long-term external debt	2,209	3,084
Public and publicly guaranteed	1,822	2,987
IMF purchases	638	631
Principal repayments	1,064	750
Long-term external debt	967	716
Public and publicly guaranteed	812	571
IMF repurchases	97	34
Net flows on external debt	1,545	2,861
Short-term external debt	−238	−104
Interest payments	353	695
Long-term external debt	325	661
Public and publicly guaranteed	285	641
IMF charges	3	10
Short-term external debt	25	23
Net transfers	1,192	2,166
Total external debt service paid	1,417	1,445
Other non-debt resource inflows		
Foreign direct investment	404	478
Portfolio equity	−382	−1,049
Major economic aggregates		
Gross national income (GNI)	41,583	48,916
Exports of goods, services and income	9,099	11,099
Workers' remittances & compensation of employees	3,363	4,155
Profit remittances on FDI	230	386
Ratios (%)		
External debt stocks to exports	189	184
External debt stocks to GNI	41	42
External debt service to exports	16	13
Present value of external debt to exports	..	156
Present value of external debt to GNI	..	37
Reserves to external debt stocks	31	35
Currency Composition (%)		
Euro	9.3	7.9
Japanese yen	29.4	28.2
U.S. dollar	42.7	47.7

St. Kitts and Nevis

Latin America & Caribbean	Upper middle income
Present value of external debt	173
Population (thousands)	52.4
External debt per capita ($)	3,868.8
Share of public sector external debt in total (%)	97.7

	2009	2010
External debt stocks	227.1	202.7
Long-term external debt	222.9	198.1
Public and publicly guaranteed	222.9	198.1
Official creditors	141.8	132.6
Private creditors	81.0	65.5
Bonds	29.1	24.1
Private nonguaranteed	0.0	0.0
Use of International Monetary Fund (IMF) credit	3.5	3.4
Short-term external debt	0.8	1.2
Interest in arrears on long-term external debt	0.8	1.2
Disbursements	9.0	7.1
Long-term external debt	5.6	7.1
Public and publicly guaranteed	5.6	7.1
IMF purchases	3.4	0.0
Principal repayments	27.2	31.4
Long-term external debt	27.2	31.4
Public and publicly guaranteed	27.2	31.4
IMF repurchases	0.0	0.0
Net flows on external debt	−18.2	−24.3
Short-term external debt	0.0	0.0
Interest payments	14.5	13.4
Long-term external debt	14.5	13.3
Public and publicly guaranteed	14.5	13.3
IMF charges	0.0	0.0
Short-term external debt	0.0	0.0
Net transfers	−32.7	−37.7
Total external debt service paid	41.7	44.8
Other non-debt resource inflows		
Foreign direct investment	130.8	128.0
Portfolio equity	..	..
Major economic aggregates		
Gross national income (GNI)	493.0	507.4
Exports of goods, services and income	196.1	192.7
Workers' remittances & compensation of employees	43.5	43.9
Profit remittances on FDI	20.3	19.3
Ratios (%)		
External debt stocks to exports	116	105
External debt stocks to GNI	46	40
External debt service to exports	21	23
Present value of external debt to exports	..	82
Present value of external debt to GNI	..	33
Reserves to external debt stocks	60	83
Currency Composition (%)		
Euro	2.4	2.4
Japanese yen	0.0	0.0
U.S. dollar	85.5	85.5

St. Lucia

Latin America & Caribbean	Upper middle income
Present value of external debt	390
Population (thousands)	174.0
External debt per capita ($)	2,664.4
Share of public sector external debt in total (%)	61.7

	2009	2010
External debt stocks	369.3	463.6
Long-term external debt	295.9	285.9
Public and publicly guaranteed	295.9	285.9
Official creditors	220.8	222.7
Private creditors	75.1	63.3
Bonds	7.8	7.8
Private nonguaranteed	0.0	0.0
Use of International Monetary Fund (IMF) credit	10.8	10.6
Short-term external debt	62.6	167.1
Interest in arrears on long-term external debt	2.6	5.1
Disbursements	21.0	21.3
Long-term external debt	10.4	21.3
Public and publicly guaranteed	10.4	21.3
IMF purchases	10.6	0.0
Principal repayments	27.3	29.6
Long-term external debt	27.3	29.6
Public and publicly guaranteed	27.3	29.6
IMF repurchases	0.0	0.0
Net flows on external debt	−460.2	93.8
Short-term external debt	−454.0	102.0
Interest payments	14.8	13.7
Long-term external debt	13.3	9.6
Public and publicly guaranteed	13.3	9.6
IMF charges	0.0	0.0
Short-term external debt	1.5	4.1
Net transfers	−475.0	80.1
Total external debt service paid	42.1	43.3
Other non-debt resource inflows		
Foreign direct investment	146.4	121.1
Portfolio equity	..	..
Major economic aggregates		
Gross national income (GNI)	872.8	857.8
Exports of goods, services and income	560.3	611.4
Workers' remittances & compensation of employees	30.5	31.4
Profit remittances on FDI	35.3	25.7
Ratios (%)		
External debt stocks to exports	66	76
External debt stocks to GNI	42	54
External debt service to exports	8	7
Present value of external debt to exports	..	68
Present value of external debt to GNI	..	44
Reserves to external debt stocks	47	44
Currency Composition (%)		
Euro	5.9	4.9
Japanese yen	0.0	0.0
U.S. dollar	69.5	70.1

St. Vincent & Grenadines

Latin America & Caribbean		Upper middle income
Present value of external debt		191
Population (thousands)		109.3
External debt per capita ($)		2,387.8
Share of public sector external debt in total (%)		97.8

	2009	2010
External debt stocks	209.6	261.1
Long-term external debt	203.2	255.3
Public and publicly guaranteed	203.2	255.3
Official creditors	143.3	206.6
Private creditors	59.8	48.7
Bonds	0.0	0.0
Private nonguaranteed	0.0	0.0
Use of International Monetary Fund (IMF) credit	5.9	5.8
Short-term external debt	0.5	0.0
Interest in arrears on long-term external debt	0.5	0.0
Disbursements	26.0	76.2
Long-term external debt	20.2	76.2
Public and publicly guaranteed	20.2	76.2
IMF purchases	5.8	0.0
Principal repayments	21.4	22.9
Long-term external debt	21.4	22.9
Public and publicly guaranteed	21.4	22.9
IMF repurchases	0.0	0.0
Net flows on external debt	4.6	53.3
Short-term external debt	0.0	0.0
Interest payments	9.8	8.7
Long-term external debt	9.7	8.7
Public and publicly guaranteed	9.7	8.7
IMF charges	0.0	0.0
Short-term external debt	0.0	0.0
Net transfers	−5.1	44.6
Total external debt service paid	31.1	31.6
Other non-debt resource inflows		
Foreign direct investment	106.1	99.7
Portfolio equity	..	..
Major economic aggregates		
Gross national income (GNI)	561.8	539.3
Exports of goods, services and income	202.8	193.1
Workers' remittances & compensation of employees	30.1	30.6
Profit remittances on FDI	12.4	10.1
Ratios (%)		
External debt stocks to exports	103	135
External debt stocks to GNI	37	48
External debt service to exports	15	16
Present value of external debt to exports	..	93
Present value of external debt to GNI	..	35
Reserves to external debt stocks	42	43
Currency Composition (%)		
Euro	5.6	3.2
Japanese yen	0.0	0.0
U.S. dollar	77.7	85.3

Sudan

Sub-Saharan Africa		Lower middle income
Present value of external debt		37,205
Population (millions)		43.6
External debt per capita ($)		501.6
Share of public sector external debt in total (%)		66.1

	2009	2010
External debt stocks	20,746	21,846
Long-term external debt	13,707	14,444
Public and publicly guaranteed	13,707	14,444
Official creditors	11,258	11,815
Private creditors	2,449	2,629
Bonds	0	0
Private nonguaranteed	0	0
Use of International Monetary Fund (IMF) credit	403	390
Short-term external debt	6,637	7,012
Interest in arrears on long-term external debt	6,420	6,658
Disbursements	971	935
Long-term external debt	971	935
Public and publicly guaranteed	971	935
IMF purchases	0	0
Principal repayments	373	403
Long-term external debt	362	397
Public and publicly guaranteed	362	397
IMF repurchases	11	6
Net flows on external debt	339	669
Short-term external debt	−259	137
Interest payments	118	89
Long-term external debt	111	83
Public and publicly guaranteed	111	83
IMF charges	0	0
Short-term external debt	7	5
Net transfers	221	580
Total external debt service paid	491	492
Other non-debt resource inflows		
Foreign direct investment	2,662	2,894
Portfolio equity	0	..
Major economic aggregates		
Gross national income (GNI)	50,018	55,939
Exports of goods, services and income	8,900	11,796
Workers' remittances & compensation of employees	2,135	1,974
Profit remittances on FDI	3,035	3,320
Ratios (%)		
External debt stocks to exports	233	185
External debt stocks to GNI	41	39
External debt service to exports	6	4
Present value of external debt to exports	..	339
Present value of external debt to GNI	..	70
Reserves to external debt stocks	5	..
Currency Composition (%)		
Euro	9.6	9.3
Japanese yen	0.6	0.7
U.S. dollar	50.5	50.8

Swaziland

Sub-Saharan Africa	Lower middle income
Present value of external debt	592
Population (millions)	1.2
External debt per capita ($)	519.2
Share of public sector external debt in total (%)	62.5

	2009	2010
External debt stocks	417.8	615.8
Long-term external debt	390.8	385.2
Public and publicly guaranteed	390.8	385.2
Official creditors	370.5	362.6
Private creditors	20.3	22.6
Bonds	0.0	0.0
Private nonguaranteed	0.0	0.0
Use of International Monetary Fund (IMF) credit	0.0	0.0
Short-term external debt	27.0	230.7
Interest in arrears on long-term external debt	25.0	35.7
Disbursements	33.2	8.0
Long-term external debt	33.2	8.0
Public and publicly guaranteed	33.2	8.0
IMF purchases	0.0	0.0
Principal repayments	28.4	26.9
Long-term external debt	28.4	26.9
Public and publicly guaranteed	28.4	26.9
IMF repurchases	0.0	0.0
Net flows on external debt	6.8	174.1
Short-term external debt	2.0	193.0
Interest payments	15.8	14.2
Long-term external debt	15.8	13.0
Public and publicly guaranteed	15.8	13.0
IMF charges	0.0	0.0
Short-term external debt	0.0	1.3
Net transfers	–9.1	159.9
Total external debt service paid	44.2	41.2
Other non-debt resource inflows		
Foreign direct investment	65.7	92.7
Portfolio equity	–6.6	..
Major economic aggregates		
Gross national income (GNI)	2,708.1	3,586.2
Exports of goods, services and income	2,150.9	..
Workers' remittances & compensation of employees	93.5	109.0
Profit remittances on FDI	352.5	..
Ratios (%)		
External debt stocks to exports	19	..
External debt stocks to GNI	15	17
External debt service to exports	2	..
Present value of external debt to exports	..	26
Present value of external debt to GNI	..	19
Reserves to external debt stocks	230	123
Currency Composition (%)		
Euro	17.6	15.6
Japanese yen	0.0	0.0
U.S. dollar	15.6	15.0

Syrian Arab Republic

Middle East & North Africa	Lower middle income
Present value of external debt	4,294
Population (millions)	20.4
External debt per capita ($)	231.3
Share of public sector external debt in total (%)	88.2

	2009	2010
External debt stocks	5,112	4,729
Long-term external debt	4,356	4,171
Public and publicly guaranteed	4,356	4,171
Official creditors	4,356	4,171
Private creditors	0	0
Bonds	0	0
Private nonguaranteed	0	0
Use of International Monetary Fund (IMF) credit	0	0
Short-term external debt	756	558
Interest in arrears on long-term external debt	206	217
Disbursements	278	286
Long-term external debt	278	286
Public and publicly guaranteed	278	286
IMF purchases	0	0
Principal repayments	489	497
Long-term external debt	489	497
Public and publicly guaranteed	489	497
IMF repurchases	0	0
Net flows on external debt	–97	–420
Short-term external debt	114	–209
Interest payments	141	133
Long-term external debt	116	110
Public and publicly guaranteed	116	110
IMF charges	0	0
Short-term external debt	25	23
Net transfers	–238	–553
Total external debt service paid	630	630
Other non-debt resource inflows		
Foreign direct investment	2,570	1,381
Portfolio equity	..	..
Major economic aggregates		
Gross national income (GNI)	52,828	57,982
Exports of goods, services and income	16,026	..
Workers' remittances & compensation of employees	1,550	1,646
Profit remittances on FDI	1,301	..
Ratios (%)		
External debt stocks to exports	32	..
External debt stocks to GNI	10	8
External debt service to exports	4	..
Present value of external debt to exports	..	23
Present value of external debt to GNI	..	8
Reserves to external debt stocks	358	436
Currency Composition (%)		
Euro	24.0	25.4
Japanese yen	14.9	15.9
U.S. dollar	31.9	29.3

Tajikistan

Europe & Central Asia	Low income
Present value of external debt	2,202
Population (millions)	6.9
External debt per capita ($)	429.6
Share of public sector external debt in total (%)	61.1

	2009	2010
External debt stocks	2,549	2,955
Long-term external debt	2,434	2,733
Public and publicly guaranteed	1,606	1,806
Official creditors	1,606	1,806
Private creditors	0	0
Bonds	0	0
Private nonguaranteed	827	927
Use of International Monetary Fund (IMF) credit	41	101
Short-term external debt	74	122
Interest in arrears on long-term external debt	0	0
Disbursements	562	951
Long-term external debt	521	892
Public and publicly guaranteed	211	249
IMF purchases	40	60
Principal repayments	426	628
Long-term external debt	411	628
Public and publicly guaranteed	35	35
IMF repurchases	15	0
Net flows on external debt	120	370
Short-term external debt	−16	47
Interest payments	42	55
Long-term external debt	41	54
Public and publicly guaranteed	24	23
IMF charges	0	0
Short-term external debt	1	1
Net transfers	77	315
Total external debt service paid	468	683
Other non-debt resource inflows		
Foreign direct investment	16	10
Portfolio equity	..	..
Major economic aggregates		
Gross national income (GNI)	4,907	5,570
Exports of goods, services and income	1,225	1,526
Workers' remittances & compensation of employees	1,748	2,254
Profit remittances on FDI	5	9
Ratios (%)		
External debt stocks to exports	208	194
External debt stocks to GNI	52	53
External debt service to exports	38	45
Present value of external debt to exports	..	146
Present value of external debt to GNI	..	42
Reserves to external debt stocks	..	..
Currency Composition (%)		
Euro	2.8	2.6
Japanese yen	0.0	0.0
U.S. dollar	82.9	81.5

Tanzania

Sub-Saharan Africa		Low income
Present value of external debt		4,947
Population (millions)		44.8
External debt per capita ($)		193.2
Share of public sector external debt in total (%)		64.3

	2009	2010
External debt stocks	7,324	8,664
Long-term external debt	5,654	6,795
Public and publicly guaranteed	4,638	5,572
Official creditors	4,521	5,459
Private creditors	118	113
Bonds	0	0
Private nonguaranteed	1,016	1,224
Use of International Monetary Fund (IMF) credit	329	354
Short-term external debt	1,341	1,515
Interest in arrears on long-term external debt	836	909
Disbursements	1,372	1,260
Long-term external debt	1,065	1,229
Public and publicly guaranteed	919	1,013
IMF purchases	307	30
Principal repayments	105	132
Long-term external debt	105	131
Public and publicly guaranteed	26	52
IMF repurchases	0	0
Net flows on external debt	1,188	1,229
Short-term external debt	−78	101
Interest payments	59	67
Long-term external debt	45	51
Public and publicly guaranteed	27	34
IMF charges	1	0
Short-term external debt	13	16
Net transfers	1,130	1,162
Total external debt service paid	164	199
Other non-debt resource inflows		
Foreign direct investment	415	433
Portfolio equity	3	3
Major economic aggregates		
Gross national income (GNI)	21,385	23,012
Exports of goods, services and income	5,274	6,552
Workers' remittances & compensation of employees	23	25
Profit remittances on FDI	184	187
Ratios (%)		
External debt stocks to exports	139	132
External debt stocks to GNI	34	38
External debt service to exports	3	3
Present value of external debt to exports	..	85
Present value of external debt to GNI	..	23
Reserves to external debt stocks	47	45
Currency Composition (%)		
Euro	4.6	3.5
Japanese yen	3.4	4.7
U.S. dollar	44.5	48.3

Thailand

East Asia & Pacific	Upper middle income
Present value of external debt	66,153
Population (millions)	69.1
External debt per capita ($)	1,031.0
Share of public sector external debt in total (%)	15.9

	2009	2010
External debt stocks	57,886	71,263
Long-term external debt	30,877	32,791
Public and publicly guaranteed	11,188	11,357
Official creditors	6,468	6,843
Private creditors	4,720	4,515
Bonds	1,754	1,954
Private nonguaranteed	19,689	21,434
Use of International Monetary Fund (IMF) credit	0	0
Short-term external debt	27,010	38,471
Interest in arrears on long-term external debt	8	2
Disbursements	9,043	10,565
Long-term external debt	9,043	10,565
Public and publicly guaranteed	866	510
IMF purchases	0	0
Principal repayments	10,911	9,661
Long-term external debt	10,911	9,661
Public and publicly guaranteed	1,188	1,168
IMF repurchases	0	0
Net flows on external debt	5,948	12,373
Short-term external debt	7,816	11,468
Interest payments	1,515	1,627
Long-term external debt	1,220	1,201
Public and publicly guaranteed	365	356
IMF charges	0	0
Short-term external debt	296	426
Net transfers	4,433	10,745
Total external debt service paid	12,427	11,288
Other non-debt resource inflows		
Foreign direct investment	4,976	6,306
Portfolio equity	1,334	3,430
Major economic aggregates		
Gross national income (GNI)	253,428	305,087
Exports of goods, services and income	186,533	233,681
Workers' remittances & compensation of employees	1,637	1,764
Profit remittances on FDI	3,402	3,403
Ratios (%)		
External debt stocks to exports	31	30
External debt stocks to GNI	23	23
External debt service to exports	7	5
Present value of external debt to exports	..	31
Present value of external debt to GNI	..	24
Reserves to external debt stocks	239	241
Currency Composition (%)		
Euro	1.9	1.6
Japanese yen	59.7	63.1
U.S. dollar	38.1	35.1

Togo

Sub-Saharan Africa		Low income
Present value of external debt		392
Population (millions)		6.0
External debt per capita ($)		286.6
Share of public sector external debt in total (%)		88.8

	2009	2010
External debt stocks	1,633	1,728
Long-term external debt	1,494	1,534
Public and publicly guaranteed	1,494	1,534
Official creditors	1,494	1,534
Private creditors	0	0
Bonds	0	0
Private nonguaranteed	0	0
Use of International Monetary Fund (IMF) credit	91	133
Short-term external debt	48	61
Interest in arrears on long-term external debt	31	32
Disbursements	76	128
Long-term external debt	35	84
Public and publicly guaranteed	35	84
IMF purchases	41	44
Principal repayments	41	26
Long-term external debt	41	26
Public and publicly guaranteed	41	26
IMF repurchases	0	0
Net flows on external debt	−33	113
Short-term external debt	−67	12
Interest payments	14	9
Long-term external debt	13	8
Public and publicly guaranteed	13	8
IMF charges	0	0
Short-term external debt	0	1
Net transfers	−46	105
Total external debt service paid	55	35
Other non-debt resource inflows		
Foreign direct investment	49	41
Portfolio equity	2	..
Major economic aggregates		
Gross national income (GNI)	2,812	2,826
Exports of goods, services and income	1,265	
Workers' remittances & compensation of employees	335	333
Profit remittances on FDI	42	..
Ratios (%)		
External debt stocks to exports	129	..
External debt stocks to GNI	58	61
External debt service to exports	4	..
Present value of external debt to exports	..	35
Present value of external debt to GNI	..	14
Reserves to external debt stocks	43	41
Currency Composition (%)		
Euro	14.8	13.1
Japanese yen	4.0	4.2
U.S. dollar	56.7	54.4

Tonga

East Asia & Pacific	Lower middle income
Present value of external debt	92
Population (thousands)	104.1
External debt per capita ($)	1,379.1
Share of public sector external debt in total (%)	100.0

	2009	2010
External debt stocks	104.6	143.5
Long-term external debt	104.6	143.5
Public and publicly guaranteed	104.6	143.5
Official creditors	103.7	142.4
Private creditors	0.9	1.1
Bonds	0.0	0.0
Private nonguaranteed	0.0	0.0
Use of International Monetary Fund (IMF) credit	0.0	0.0
Short-term external debt	0.0	0.0
Interest in arrears on long-term external debt	0.0	0.0
Disbursements	17.4	40.9
Long-term external debt	17.4	40.9
Public and publicly guaranteed	17.4	40.9
IMF purchases	0.0	0.0
Principal repayments	2.4	2.7
Long-term external debt	2.4	2.7
Public and publicly guaranteed	2.4	2.7
IMF repurchases	0.0	0.0
Net flows on external debt	14.9	38.2
Short-term external debt	0.0	0.0
Interest payments	1.4	2.3
Long-term external debt	1.4	2.3
Public and publicly guaranteed	1.4	2.3
IMF charges	0.0	0.0
Short-term external debt	0.0	0.0
Net transfers	13.5	35.9
Total external debt service paid	3.8	5.0
Other non-debt resource inflows		
Foreign direct investment	−0.0	16.2
Portfolio equity	..	..
Major economic aggregates		
Gross national income (GNI)	332.6	361.7
Exports of goods, services and income	53.6	54.9
Workers' remittances & compensation of employees	71.5	84.6
Profit remittances on FDI	0.0	..
Ratios (%)		
External debt stocks to exports	195	261
External debt stocks to GNI	31	40
External debt service to exports	7	9
Present value of external debt to exports	..	167
Present value of external debt to GNI	..	26
Reserves to external debt stocks	92	73
Currency Composition (%)		
Euro	0.1	0.0
Japanese yen	0.0	0.0
U.S. dollar	30.3	21.4

Tunisia

Middle East & North Africa	Upper middle income
Present value of external debt	19,307
Population (millions)	10.5
External debt per capita ($)	2,046.1
Share of public sector external debt in total (%)	66.8

	2009	2010
External debt stocks	21,711	21,584
Long-term external debt	16,910	16,605
Public and publicly guaranteed	14,840	14,609
Official creditors	9,960	10,158
Private creditors	4,880	4,452
Bonds	3,776	3,819
Private nonguaranteed	2,070	1,996
Use of International Monetary Fund (IMF) credit	0	0
Short-term external debt	4,801	4,979
Interest in arrears on long-term external debt	0	0
Disbursements	1,547	1,714
Long-term external debt	1,547	1,714
Public and publicly guaranteed	1,367	1,540
IMF purchases	0	0
Principal repayments	1,347	1,633
Long-term external debt	1,347	1,633
Public and publicly guaranteed	1,230	1,385
IMF repurchases	0	0
Net flows on external debt	675	258
Short-term external debt	474	177
Interest payments	758	716
Long-term external debt	700	647
Public and publicly guaranteed	598	546
IMF charges	0	0
Short-term external debt	58	68
Net transfers	-83	-458
Total external debt service paid	2,105	2,349
Other non-debt resource inflows		
Foreign direct investment	1,595	1,401
Portfolio equity	-89	-26
Major economic aggregates		
Gross national income (GNI)	41,240	42,242
Exports of goods, services and income	20,235	22,667
Workers' remittances & compensation of employees	1,964	1,970
Profit remittances on FDI	1,588	1,658
Ratios (%)		
External debt stocks to exports	107	95
External debt stocks to GNI	53	51
External debt service to exports	10	10
Present value of external debt to exports	..	77
Present value of external debt to GNI	..	47
Reserves to external debt stocks	52	45
Currency Composition (%)		
Euro	49.0	49.1
Japanese yen	18.5	18.2
U.S. dollar	12.5	12.0

Turkey

Europe & Central Asia	Upper middle income
Present value of external debt	270,204
Population (millions)	72.8
External debt per capita ($)	4,039.4
Share of public sector external debt in total (%)	31.2

	2009	2010
External debt stocks	271,225	293,872
Long-term external debt	213,555	210,123
Public and publicly guaranteed	87,083	93,088
Official creditors	23,128	26,504
Private creditors	63,956	66,584
Bonds	43,058	46,276
Private nonguaranteed	126,472	117,035
Use of International Monetary Fund (IMF) credit	7,958	5,627
Short-term external debt	49,711	78,123
Interest in arrears on long-term external debt	0	0
Disbursements	39,605	46,499
Long-term external debt	39,605	46,499
Public and publicly guaranteed	9,866	14,637
IMF purchases	0	0
Principal repayments	50,013	47,187
Long-term external debt	49,307	45,016
Public and publicly guaranteed	6,469	5,959
IMF repurchases	706	2,171
Net flows on external debt	–13,801	27,724
Short-term external debt	–3,393	28,412
Interest payments	12,226	11,501
Long-term external debt	10,295	8,637
Public and publicly guaranteed	4,945	4,684
IMF charges	192	130
Short-term external debt	1,740	2,734
Net transfers	–26,027	16,222
Total external debt service paid	62,239	58,688
Other non-debt resource inflows		
Foreign direct investment	8,409	9,278
Portfolio equity	2,827	3,468
Major economic aggregates		
Gross national income (GNI)	606,365	727,445
Exports of goods, services and income	148,466	159,736
Workers' remittances & compensation of employees	970	874
Profit remittances on FDI	2,914	3,044
Ratios (%)		
External debt stocks to exports	183	184
External debt stocks to GNI	45	40
External debt service to exports	42	37
Present value of external debt to exports	..	165
Present value of external debt to GNI	..	39
Reserves to external debt stocks	28	29
Currency Composition (%)		
Euro	29.5	31.1
Japanese yen	3.7	4.5
U.S. dollar	66.1	63.8

Turkmenistan

Europe & Central Asia		Lower middle income
Present value of external debt		380
Population (millions)		5.0
External debt per capita ($)		83.6
Share of public sector external debt in total (%)		85.3

	2009	2010
External debt stocks	552.0	421.6
Long-term external debt	477.2	366.8
Public and publicly guaranteed	463.3	359.5
Official creditors	409.5	341.6
Private creditors	53.9	17.8
Bonds	0.0	0.0
Private nonguaranteed	13.9	7.4
Use of International Monetary Fund (IMF) credit	0.0	0.0
Short-term external debt	74.8	54.8
Interest in arrears on long-term external debt	0.8	0.8
Disbursements	35.2	25.5
Long-term external debt	35.2	25.5
Public and publicly guaranteed	22.4	17.9
IMF purchases	0.0	0.0
Principal repayments	146.4	142.8
Long-term external debt	146.4	142.8
Public and publicly guaranteed	146.4	129.8
IMF repurchases	0.0	0.0
Net flows on external debt	−87.2	−137.4
Short-term external debt	24.0	−20.0
Interest payments	18.6	11.5
Long-term external debt	17.6	10.8
Public and publicly guaranteed	17.1	10.3
IMF charges	0.0	0.0
Short-term external debt	1.0	0.8
Net transfers	−105.8	−148.9
Total external debt service paid	165.0	154.4
Other non-debt resource inflows		
Foreign direct investment	3,867.0	2,083.0
Portfolio equity	..	..
Major economic aggregates		
Gross national income (GNI)	17,177.8	19,774.0
Exports of goods, services and income	..	..
Workers' remittances & compensation of employees	..	..
Profit remittances on FDI	..	..
Ratios (%)		
External debt stocks to exports	..	..
External debt stocks to GNI	3	2
External debt service to exports	..	..
Present value of external debt to exports	..	2
Present value of external debt to GNI	..	2
Reserves to external debt stocks	..	..
Currency Composition (%)		
Euro	32.5	29.1
Japanese yen	33.4	28.9
U.S. dollar	6.4	3.6

Uganda

Sub-Saharan Africa		Low income
Present value of external debt		1,100
Population (millions)		33.4
External debt per capita ($)		89.6
Share of public sector external debt in total (%)		89.1

	2009	2010
External debt stocks	2,465	2,994
Long-term external debt	2,221	2,671
Public and publicly guaranteed	2,221	2,671
Official creditors	2,220	2,671
Private creditors	0	0
Bonds	0	0
Private nonguaranteed	0	0
Use of International Monetary Fund (IMF) credit	9	9
Short-term external debt	235	314
Interest in arrears on long-term external debt	26	26
Disbursements	493	486
Long-term external debt	493	486
Public and publicly guaranteed	493	486
IMF purchases	0	0
Principal repayments	49	40
Long-term external debt	49	40
Public and publicly guaranteed	49	40
IMF repurchases	0	0
Net flows on external debt	221	525
Short-term external debt	−223	79
Interest payments	22	24
Long-term external debt	18	21
Public and publicly guaranteed	18	21
IMF charges	0	0
Short-term external debt	4	3
Net transfers	199	501
Total external debt service paid	71	64
Other non-debt resource inflows		
Foreign direct investment	789	817
Portfolio equity	131	−70
Major economic aggregates		
Gross national income (GNI)	15,516	16,720
Exports of goods, services and income	3,335	3,494
Workers' remittances & compensation of employees	778	915
Profit remittances on FDI	164	192
Ratios (%)		
External debt stocks to exports	74	86
External debt stocks to GNI	16	18
External debt service to exports	2	2
Present value of external debt to exports	..	33
Present value of external debt to GNI	..	7
Reserves to external debt stocks	121	95
Currency Composition (%)		
Euro	5.1	3.4
Japanese yen	0.5	0.8
U.S. dollar	47.6	47.2

Ukraine

Europe & Central Asia		Lower middle income
Present value of external debt		107,452
Population (millions)		45.9
External debt per capita ($)		2,546.5
Share of public sector external debt in total (%)		13.9

	2009	2010
External debt stocks	103,435	116,808
Long-term external debt	72,587	76,104
Public and publicly guaranteed	13,482	16,246
Official creditors	6,026	5,789
Private creditors	7,455	10,456
Bonds	5,907	9,148
Private nonguaranteed	59,106	59,858
Use of International Monetary Fund (IMF) credit	10,974	14,245
Short-term external debt	19,873	26,459
Interest in arrears on long-term external debt	650	866
Disbursements	22,600	38,932
Long-term external debt	16,430	35,499
Public and publicly guaranteed	664	3,998
IMF purchases	6,170	3,433
Principal repayments	18,232	25,672
Long-term external debt	18,143	25,672
Public and publicly guaranteed	1,942	1,107
IMF repurchases	88	0
Net flows on external debt	3,291	19,630
Short-term external debt	–1,078	6,370
Interest payments	4,591	4,429
Long-term external debt	4,200	3,835
Public and publicly guaranteed	696	469
IMF charges	135	241
Short-term external debt	256	353
Net transfers	–1,300	15,201
Total external debt service paid	22,823	30,101
Other non-debt resource inflows		
Foreign direct investment	4,816	6,495
Portfolio equity	105	290
Major economic aggregates		
Gross national income (GNI)	114,788	135,987
Exports of goods, services and income	58,877	73,970
Workers' remittances & compensation of employees	5,073	5,607
Profit remittances on FDI	2,542	2,218
Ratios (%)		
External debt stocks to exports	176	158
External debt stocks to GNI	90	86
External debt service to exports	39	41
Present value of external debt to exports	..	144
Present value of external debt to GNI	..	75
Reserves to external debt stocks	26	30
Currency Composition (%)		
Euro	17.0	13.3
Japanese yen	3.6	0.9
U.S. dollar	75.6	83.5

Uruguay

Latin America & Caribbean	Upper middle income
Present value of external debt	10,234
Population (millions)	3.4
External debt per capita ($)	3,380.6
Share of public sector external debt in total (%)	85.5

	2009	2010
External debt stocks	11,131	11,347
Long-term external debt	10,007	9,797
Public and publicly guaranteed	9,927	9,704
Official creditors	3,790	3,611
Private creditors	6,138	6,093
Bonds	6,071	6,021
Private nonguaranteed	80	93
Use of International Monetary Fund (IMF) credit	0	0
Short-term external debt	1,124	1,550
Interest in arrears on long-term external debt	0	0
Disbursements	1,575	417
Long-term external debt	1,575	417
Public and publicly guaranteed	1,575	417
IMF purchases	0	0
Principal repayments	534	700
Long-term external debt	534	700
Public and publicly guaranteed	434	700
IMF repurchases	0	0
Net flows on external debt	1,348	144
Short-term external debt	307	426
Interest payments	446	670
Long-term external debt	395	599
Public and publicly guaranteed	384	592
IMF charges	0	0
Short-term external debt	51	71
Net transfers	902	−527
Total external debt service paid	979	1,370
Other non-debt resource inflows		
Foreign direct investment	1,262	1,827
Portfolio equity	−12	−12
Major economic aggregates		
Gross national income (GNI)	30,651	39,162
Exports of goods, services and income	9,070	11,020
Workers' remittances & compensation of employees	101	103
Profit remittances on FDI	401	730
Ratios (%)		
External debt stocks to exports	123	103
External debt stocks to GNI	36	29
External debt service to exports	11	12
Present value of external debt to exports	..	102
Present value of external debt to GNI	..	31
Reserves to external debt stocks	72	67
Currency Composition (%)		
Euro	5.0	4.7
Japanese yen	5.1	5.6
U.S. dollar	87.8	89.3

Uzbekistan

Europe & Central Asia	Lower middle income
Present value of external debt	5,972
Population (millions)	28.2
External debt per capita ($)	262.9
Share of public sector external debt in total (%)	46.2

	2009	2010
External debt stocks	6,550	7,404
Long-term external debt	6,386	7,167
Public and publicly guaranteed	3,246	3,426
Official creditors	2,912	3,173
Private creditors	333	252
Bonds	0	0
Private nonguaranteed	3,141	3,741
Use of International Monetary Fund (IMF) credit	0	0
Short-term external debt	163	238
Interest in arrears on long-term external debt	19	70
Disbursements	2,633	1,183
Long-term external debt	2,633	1,183
Public and publicly guaranteed	481	447
IMF purchases	0	0
Principal repayments	717	471
Long-term external debt	717	471
Public and publicly guaranteed	383	340
IMF repurchases	0	0
Net flows on external debt	1,849	737
Short-term external debt	−67	24
Interest payments	123	124
Long-term external debt	120	118
Public and publicly guaranteed	82	62
IMF charges	0	0
Short-term external debt	2	6
Net transfers	1,726	613
Total external debt service paid	840	595
Other non-debt resource inflows		
Foreign direct investment	711	822
Portfolio equity	..	..
Major economic aggregates		
Gross national income (GNI)	32,636	39,013
Exports of goods, services and income	..	..
Workers' remittances & compensation of employees	..	..
Profit remittances on FDI	..	..
Ratios (%)		
External debt stocks to exports	..	..
External debt stocks to GNI	20	19
External debt service to exports	..	..
Present value of external debt to exports	..	45
Present value of external debt to GNI	..	18
Reserves to external debt stocks	..	..
Currency Composition (%)		
Euro	12.6	10.4
Japanese yen	23.8	22.7
U.S. dollar	53.0	54.5

Vanuatu

East Asia & Pacific	Lower middle income
Present value of external debt	113
Population (thousands)	239.7
External debt per capita ($)	618.7
Share of public sector external debt in total (%)	67.0

	2009	2010
External debt stocks	129.8	148.3
Long-term external debt	98.8	99.3
Public and publicly guaranteed	98.8	99.3
Official creditors	98.8	99.3
Private creditors	0.0	0.0
Bonds	0.0	0.0
Private nonguaranteed	0.0	0.0
Use of International Monetary Fund (IMF) credit	0.0	0.0
Short-term external debt	31.0	49.0
Interest in arrears on long-term external debt	0.0	0.0
Disbursements	11.7	0.0
Long-term external debt	11.7	0.0
Public and publicly guaranteed	11.7	0.0
IMF purchases	0.0	0.0
Principal repayments	3.5	3.6
Long-term external debt	3.5	3.6
Public and publicly guaranteed	3.5	3.6
IMF repurchases	0.0	0.0
Net flows on external debt	3.1	14.4
Short-term external debt	−5.0	18.0
Interest payments	2.1	2.3
Long-term external debt	1.4	1.4
Public and publicly guaranteed	1.4	1.4
IMF charges	0.0	0.0
Short-term external debt	0.7	0.9
Net transfers	1.0	12.1
Total external debt service paid	5.6	5.9
Other non-debt resource inflows		
Foreign direct investment	32.1	38.9
Portfolio equity	..	..
Major economic aggregates		
Gross national income (GNI)	593.8	708.6
Exports of goods, services and income	329.1	356.1
Workers' remittances & compensation of employees	5.5	6.4
Profit remittances on FDI	..	..
Ratios (%)		
External debt stocks to exports	39	42
External debt stocks to GNI	22	21
External debt service to exports	2	2
Present value of external debt to exports	..	41
Present value of external debt to GNI	..	18
Reserves to external debt stocks	114	109
Currency Composition (%)		
Euro	7.1	5.2
Japanese yen	0.0	0.0
U.S. dollar	41.6	42.3

Venezuela, RB

Latin America & Caribbean	Upper middle income
Present value of external debt	55,591
Population (millions)	28.8
External debt per capita ($)	1,927.3
Share of public sector external debt in total (%)	66.7

	2009	2010
External debt stocks	55,235	55,572
Long-term external debt	38,493	40,146
Public and publicly guaranteed	35,183	37,086
Official creditors	4,130	4,957
Private creditors	31,053	32,129
Bonds	28,360	29,762
Private nonguaranteed	3,310	3,060
Use of International Monetary Fund (IMF) credit	0	0
Short-term external debt	16,741	15,426
Interest in arrears on long-term external debt	7	7
Disbursements	6,068	4,317
Long-term external debt	6,068	4,317
Public and publicly guaranteed	6,068	4,317
IMF purchases	0	0
Principal repayments	812	2,623
Long-term external debt	812	2,623
Public and publicly guaranteed	812	2,373
IMF repurchases	0	0
Net flows on external debt	2,424	378
Short-term external debt	-2,832	-1,315
Interest payments	3,170	3,462
Long-term external debt	2,765	3,088
Public and publicly guaranteed	2,440	2,787
IMF charges	0	0
Short-term external debt	406	374
Net transfers	-747	-3,083
Total external debt service paid	3,983	6,085
Other non-debt resource inflows		
Foreign direct investment	-3,105	-1,404
Portfolio equity	121	8
Major economic aggregates		
Gross national income (GNI)	323,481	387,566
Exports of goods, services and income	61,913	69,450
Workers' remittances & compensation of employees	131	143
Profit remittances on FDI	1,903	1,955
Ratios (%)		
External debt stocks to exports	89	80
External debt stocks to GNI	17	14
External debt service to exports	6	9
Present value of external debt to exports	..	70
Present value of external debt to GNI	..	16
Reserves to external debt stocks	62	53
Currency Composition (%)		
Euro	6.7	5.9
Japanese yen	0.8	0.4
U.S. dollar	91.0	92.6

Vietnam

East Asia & Pacific	Lower middle income
Present value of external debt	26,565
Population (millions)	86.9
External debt per capita ($)	404.2
Share of public sector external debt in total (%)	80.1

	2009	2010
External debt stocks	28,718	35,139
Long-term external debt	23,447	28,145
Public and publicly guaranteed	23,447	28,145
Official creditors	21,643	25,255
Private creditors	1,805	2,890
Bonds	1,038	2,020
Private nonguaranteed	0	0
Use of International Monetary Fund (IMF) credit	84	45
Short-term external debt	5,186	6,949
Interest in arrears on long-term external debt	0	0
Disbursements	3,891	4,437
Long-term external debt	3,891	4,437
Public and publicly guaranteed	3,891	4,437
IMF purchases	0	0
Principal repayments	781	851
Long-term external debt	743	813
Public and publicly guaranteed	743	813
IMF repurchases	38	38
Net flows on external debt	4,017	5,348
Short-term external debt	908	1,763
Interest payments	435	521
Long-term external debt	374	442
Public and publicly guaranteed	374	442
IMF charges	1	0
Short-term external debt	61	79
Net transfers	3,582	4,828
Total external debt service paid	1,217	1,372
Other non-debt resource inflows		
Foreign direct investment	7,600	8,000
Portfolio equity	128	2,383
Major economic aggregates		
Gross national income (GNI)	91,826	96,322
Exports of goods, services and income	63,615	80,108
Workers' remittances & compensation of employees	6,840	8,000
Profit remittances on FDI	..	..
Ratios (%)		
External debt stocks to exports	45	44
External debt stocks to GNI	31	36
External debt service to exports	2	2
Present value of external debt to exports	..	37
Present value of external debt to GNI	..	29
Reserves to external debt stocks	57	35
Currency Composition (%)		
Euro	5.5	4.9
Japanese yen	35.5	36.0
U.S. dollar	39.2	41.2

Yemen, Rep.

Middle East & North Africa		Lower middle income
Present value of external debt		3,971
Population (millions)		24.1
External debt per capita ($)		262.9
Share of public sector external debt in total (%)		93.8

	2009	2010
External debt stocks	6,370	6,324
Long-term external debt	5,875	5,933
Public and publicly guaranteed	5,875	5,933
Official creditors	5,871	5,930
Private creditors	5	3
Bonds	0	0
Private nonguaranteed	0	0
Use of International Monetary Fund (IMF) credit	53	78
Short-term external debt	442	313
Interest in arrears on long-term external debt	117	124
Disbursements	332	340
Long-term external debt	332	287
Public and publicly guaranteed	332	287
IMF purchases	0	53
Principal repayments	184	182
Long-term external debt	140	155
Public and publicly guaranteed	140	155
IMF repurchases	44	27
Net flows on external debt	102	22
Short-term external debt	−46	−136
Interest payments	79	78
Long-term external debt	72	74
Public and publicly guaranteed	72	74
IMF charges	0	0
Short-term external debt	6	4
Net transfers	23	−55
Total external debt service paid	263	259
Other non-debt resource inflows		
Foreign direct investment	129	−329
Portfolio equity	0	0
Major economic aggregates		
Gross national income (GNI)	24,894	..
Exports of goods, services and income	7,207	9,390
Workers' remittances & compensation of employees	1,160	1,240
Profit remittances on FDI	927	..
Ratios (%)		
External debt stocks to exports	88	67
External debt stocks to GNI	26	..
External debt service to exports	4	3
Present value of external debt to exports	..	44
Present value of external debt to GNI	..	15
Reserves to external debt stocks	110	94
Currency Composition (%)		
Euro	1.9	1.8
Japanese yen	5.8	5.1
U.S. dollar	58.8	57.3

Zambia

Sub-Saharan Africa	Lower middle income
Present value of external debt	1,561
Population (millions)	12.9
External debt per capita ($)	285.4
Share of public sector external debt in total (%)	35.5

	2009	2010
External debt stocks	3,039	3,689
Long-term external debt	2,220	2,104
Public and publicly guaranteed	1,200	1,309
Official creditors	1,158	1,276
Private creditors	42	33
Bonds	0	0
Private nonguaranteed	1,020	794
Use of International Monetary Fund (IMF) credit	345	395
Short-term external debt	474	1,191
Interest in arrears on long-term external debt	154	167
Disbursements	369	251
Long-term external debt	126	195
Public and publicly guaranteed	91	168
IMF purchases	244	56
Principal repayments	122	87
Long-term external debt	122	86
Public and publicly guaranteed	59	47
IMF repurchases	0	1
Net flows on external debt	45	868
Short-term external debt	−202	704
Interest payments	47	60
Long-term external debt	36	29
Public and publicly guaranteed	13	11
IMF charges	1	0
Short-term external debt	10	31
Net transfers	−2	808
Total external debt service paid	169	147
Other non-debt resource inflows		
Foreign direct investment	695	1,041
Portfolio equity	−13	101
Major economic aggregates		
Gross national income (GNI)	11,442	14,300
Exports of goods, services and income	4,564	7,734
Workers' remittances & compensation of employees	41	44
Profit remittances on FDI	265	1,832
Ratios (%)		
External debt stocks to exports	67	48
External debt stocks to GNI	27	26
External debt service to exports	4	2
Present value of external debt to exports	..	27
Present value of external debt to GNI	..	12
Reserves to external debt stocks	62	57
Currency Composition (%)		
Euro	13.3	10.6
Japanese yen	0.0	0.1
U.S. dollar	37.4	34.0

Zimbabwe

Sub-Saharan Africa		Low income
Present value of external debt		6,001
Population (millions)		12.6
External debt per capita ($)		399.0
Share of public sector external debt in total (%)		73.5

	2009	2010
External debt stocks	4,801	5,016
Long-term external debt	3,831	4,064
Public and publicly guaranteed	3,742	3,686
Official creditors	3,296	3,253
Private creditors	446	432
Bonds	0	0
Private nonguaranteed	89	378
Use of International Monetary Fund (IMF) credit	116	110
Short-term external debt	854	843
Interest in arrears on long-term external debt	707	706
Disbursements	79	369
Long-term external debt	79	369
Public and publicly guaranteed	13	20
IMF purchases	0	0
Principal repayments	66	66
Long-term external debt	66	62
Public and publicly guaranteed	0	1
IMF repurchases	0	4
Net flows on external debt	−431	293
Short-term external debt	−444	−10
Interest payments	35	43
Long-term external debt	30	41
Public and publicly guaranteed	14	13
IMF charges	0	0
Short-term external debt	5	2
Net transfers	−466	251
Total external debt service paid	101	109
Other non-debt resource inflows		
Foreign direct investment	105	105
Portfolio equity	..	..
Major economic aggregates		
Gross national income (GNI)	5,394	6,988
Exports of goods, services and income	..	..
Workers' remittances & compensation of employees	..	..
Profit remittances on FDI	..	..
Ratios (%)		
External debt stocks to exports	..	..
External debt stocks to GNI	89	72
External debt service to exports	..	..
Present value of external debt to exports	..	275
Present value of external debt to GNI	..	110
Reserves to external debt stocks	..	..
Currency Composition (%)		
Euro	33.4	31.9
Japanese yen	5.8	6.7
U.S. dollar	29.9	30.1

Glossary

Bonds are debt instruments issued by public and publicly guaranteed or private debtors with duration of one year or longer. Bonds usually give the holder the unconditional right to fixed money income or contractually determined, variable money income.

Currency composition of public and publicly guaranteed debt provides information on the share of loans outstanding and disbursed by currency of repayment. For major multilateral creditors, the currency composition of the relevant unit of account is also taken into account. The principal currencies in which the external debt of low-and middle-income countries is contracted (the Euro, Japanese yen, and U.S. dollar) are separately identified. Beginning in 2001, debt denominated in the currencies of the members in the euro area is included under the euro rather than the national currencies that previously prevailed.

Disbursements are drawings during the year specified on loan commitments contracted by the borrower.

Exports of goods, services, and income constitute the total value of exports of goods and services, receipts of compensation of nonresident workers, and investment income from abroad.

External debt per capita is total external debt divided by midyear population.

External debt ratios are ratios of debt and debt service to selected economic aggregates.

External debt service to exports, also called the external debt service ratio, is the ratio of external debt service paid to exports of goods and services.

External debt stocks comprise public and publicly guaranteed long-term external debt, private nonguaranteed long-term external debt, use of IMF credit, and short-term external debt, including interest arrears on long-term debt.

External debt stocks to exports is the ratio of outstanding external debt to the value of exports of goods and services and receipts of income from abroad.

External debt stocks to GNI is the ratio of outstanding external debt to gross national income.

Foreign direct investment, net refers to direct investment flows in the reporting economy. It is the sum of equity capital, reinvestment earnings and other capital. The term describes a category of international investment made by a resident entity in one economy (direct investor) with the objective of establishing a lasting interest in an enterprise resident in an economy other than that of the investor (direct investment enterprise). Ownership of 10 percent or more of the ordinary shares or voting stock is the criterion for determining the existence of a direct investment relationship.

Glossary

Gross national income (GNI) is the sum of value added by all resident producers plus any product taxes (less subsidies) not included in the valuation of output, plus net receipts of primary income (compensation of employees and property income) from abroad. Yearly average exchange rates are used to convert GNI from local currency to U.S. dollars.

International Monetary Fund (IMF) charges are the amounts of interest paid in foreign currency in the year specified for transactions with the IMF.

International Monetary Fund (IMF) purchases are the total drawings on the general resources account of the IMF during the year specified, excluding drawings in the reserve tranche.

International Monetary Fund (IMF) repurchases are the amounts of principal (amortization) paid in foreign currency in the year specified for transactions with the IMF.

Interest in arrears on long-term external debt are interest payments due but not paid, shown on a cumulative basis. Interest arrears are due and payable immediately and are therefore regarded as short-term obligations. Thus, an increase in interest arrears on long-term debt will be recorded as an increase in short-term debt. Interest in arrears on the use of IMF credit is also considered to be part of short-term external debt.

Interest payments are the amount of interest paid in foreign currency, goods, or services in the year specified.

Long-term external debt is debt that has an original or extended maturity of more than one year and that is owed to nonresidents by residents of an economy and repayable in foreign currency, goods, or services.

Net flows on external debt are disbursements on long-term external debt and IMF purchases minus principal repayments on long-term external debt and IMF repurchases.

Net transfers are net flows minus interest payments.

Official creditors are governments or other bilateral public entities, such as export-import agencies, development agencies, and multilateral financial institutions, such as the World Bank and regional development banks.

Population is the midyear estimate of all residents regardless of legal status or citizenship, except for refugees not permanently settled in the country of asylum, who are generally considered part of the population of their country of origin.

Portfolio equity flows is the category of international investment that covers investment in equity securities. Equity securities include shares, stocks, participation, or similar documents (such as American Depositary Receipts) that usually denote ownership of equity.

Glossary

Present value of external debt outstanding is the nominal value of all future debt service obligations on existing debt discounted at prevailing market rates of interest. The interest rates used in this calculation are the Commercial Interest Reference Rates (CIRR) for each relevant currency compiled and published by the Organisation for Economic Co-operation and Development.

Present value of external debt to exports is the ratio of the present value of external debt to exports of goods and services. It is calculated as the ratio of the present value of external debt for 2010 to the three-year (2008–10) average of exports and might include World Bank staff estimates.

Present value of external debt to GNI is the ratio of the present value of external debt to gross national income (GNI). It is calculated as the ratio of the present value of external debt for 2010 to the three-year (2008–10) average of GNI and might include World Bank staff estimates.

Principal repayments are the amounts of principal (amortization) paid in foreign currency, goods, or services.

Private creditors are bondholders, commercial banks, and other trade-related lenders.

Private nonguaranteed debt is debt owed by private sector borrowers to external creditors on loans that do not benefit from a public sector guarantee by the debtor country.

Profit remittances on FDI are payments of direct investment income (debit side), which consist of income on equity (dividends, branch profits, and reinvested earnings) and income on intercompany debt (interest).

Public and publicly guaranteed debt comprises public debt (an external obligation of a public debtor, such as the national government or agency, a political subdivision or agency, or an autonomous public body) and publicly guaranteed external debt (an external obligation of a private debtor that is guaranteed for repayment by a public entity).

Reserves to external debt stocks is the ratio of international reserves to outstanding external debt.

Share of public sector external debt in total is public sector external debt as a percentage of total external debt.

Short-term external debt has an original maturity of one year or less. Available data permit no distinction between public and private nonguaranteed short-term external debt.

Total external debt service paid is debt service payments on long-term external debt (public and publicly guaranteed and private nonguaranteed), use of International Monetary Fund credit, and interest on short-term external debt.

Glossary

Use of International Monetary Fund (IMF) credit denotes members' drawings on the IMF other than amounts drawn against the country's reserve tranche position. Use of IMF credit includes purchases and drawings under Stand-By, Extended, Structural Adjustment, Enhanced Structural Adjustment, and Systemic Transformation Facility Arrangements, as well as Trust Fund Loans.

Workers' remittances & compensation of employees constitute the sum of worker's remittances, compensation of employees, and migrants' transfers as defined in the IMF's *Balance of Payments Manual* (BPM5).